BFI Modern Classics

Rob White
Series Editor

BFI Modern Classics is a series of critical studies of films produced over the last three decades. Writers explore their chosen films, offering a range of perspectives on the dominant art and entertainment medium in contemporary culture. The series gathers together snapshots of our passion for and understanding of recent movies.

Distant Voices, Still Lives

Paul Farley

 Publishing

For Thelma Irene Farley

First published in 2006 by the
British Film Institute
21 Stephen Street, London W1T 1LN

The British Film Institute's purpose is to
champion moving image culture in all
its richness and diversity across the UK,
for the benefit of as wide an audience as
possible, and to create and encourage
debate.

Series design by Andrew Barron
& Collis Clements Associates

Typeset in Italian Garamond
and Swiss 721BT by
D R Bungay Associates,
Burghfield, Berks

Printed in the UK by
Cromwell Press, Trowbridge, Wiltshire

British Library Cataloguing-in-Publication Data

A catalogue record for this book is available
from the British Library

ISBN 1–84457–139–4

Contents

Acknowledgments

Terence Davies has been the most generous and gracious supporter of this project imaginable. Rob White first thought it might be interesting to let a poet write on this film; Rebecca Barden and Tom Cabot saw it through. Annette Kuhn, Grevel Lindop and Kevin Watson all helped me look (and listen) again. Carole Romaya watched the film many times with me, and Geoff Andrew provided invaluable notes on the manuscript. In many ways the singular vision that brought us *Distant Voices, Still Lives* was the product of a state-supported arts education and film sector, which I'm also partly a product of: at Chelsea School of Art in the mid-1980s, while Davies was making his film, I was trying to paint interiors lit with the light of childhood on a grant from Liverpool City Council but was almost led astray into film on several occasions thanks to the enthusiasms of Anna Thew, who introduced me to the work of Maya Deren, Kenneth Anger, Andy Warhol, Michael Snow, Bruce Baillie and many others with the kind of straightforward passion that can last a lifetime.

Introduction

'Where does memory end, and imagination begin?'
Terence Davies[1]

I'm standing on the other side of an age in which the world went from
black and white to colour. I'm looking back towards the old port city of my
birth, lashed by broad Atlantic fronts always moving in from the west. Rain
is falling on back entries and nit nurses and the old parquet floor of Clint
Road Infants. I'm looking back across a chasm flooded with Day-Glo,
where stereo pans from speaker to speaker and crisps come in dozens of
different flavours. I'm crossing Wavertree Road again, back to the earthy,
yeasty cellar smells of the pubs opening, the rag-and-bone man's long
abraded cry, the crumbling ceiling roses and lost wallpaper and bare light
bulbs, and beyond. I can date this fairly accurately, because Louis
Armstrong is always singing 'What a Wonderful World' on the wireless:
it's the spring of 1968, the very edge of my memory.

We should go in fear of writing about things we admire. It's a
dangerous business. The temptation, when faced with such a thing, is to
quote and enthuse at length, to lather it with adjectives, but the harder

you gush, the more asthenic the prose. I've tried to trick myself out of this law of inverse ratio by concentrating on a few aspects of Terence Davies's *Distant Voices, Still Lives* – a film I've loved and respected since first seeing it seventeen years ago – in the hope that a few ideas might emerge and eddy around each of these distinct areas. I also thought it only right to approach a film made up of, and built from, 'a pattern of timeless moments'[2] in such a mosaic fashion.

Distant Voices, Still Lives went on general release in the UK in the autumn of 1988, but began life, as many films do, a long time before. Terence Davies was born in Liverpool on 10 November 1945, the youngest of seven children. His father died when he was six years old after a long illness, and from then on Davies grew up in a household consisting of his mother and elder siblings. Instead of entering higher education, Davies did what many of his class and generation did: he left school at fifteen to work. Over the next twelve years he did so, first as an articled clerk and then a book-keeper in a Liverpool office, before moving to Coventry in 1972 to study at drama school. While there, Davies wrote his first screenplay, *Children*, and was given the opportunity to direct it following an award from the British Film Institute. He then studied at the National Film School in London, where he made the second part of what was to become his *Trilogy*: *Madonna and Child*. The third film, *Death and Transfiguration*, completed the piece, which went on to receive international acclaim and recognition for its director.

These are the bare biographical bones that bring us to *Distant Voices, Still Lives* – actually two films, made separately in 1986 and 1988, which connect with each other and interpenetrate – though the story is of course much more detailed, much richer. The film was well received on its release, and indeed proved Davies's breakthrough: it took the International Critics Prize at Cannes, garnered very favourable critical reviews and easily became the art-house hit of that year. There was a magical sense of it having come from nowhere (unless you already knew the *Trilogy*), and of looking like nothing else. When *The Long Day Closes* appeared in 1992, it became clear how all of Davies's work up until that point constituted a larger autobiographical cycle. Since then he has directed two more films: 1995's *The Neon Bible* (based on the book by

John Kennedy Toole) and in 2000 a version of Edith Wharton's *The House of Mirth*. There is also Davies's work in other mediums to consider: in 1984 he published a novel, *Hallelujah Now*, which itself provides considerable echoes when read in the light of the films; he has also written a radio play, *The Walk to the Paradise Garden*, which was produced and broadcast on BBC radio in 2001.

While I was thinking about writing this book in the damp summer of 2004, a maternal uncle I didn't know I had was knocked over and killed at a pedestrian crossing in Picton Road, Liverpool. My mother and father's families all lived in this area once, within a couple of miles of each other. This is where I was born and spent my first few years. Davies's own childhood places fall within this ambit, too. As I was trying to figure out a way of mourning a relative who I never even knew existed, the bad news started up what I can only describe as an old ache. I began thinking a lot about that part of the city, its sandstone that the rain turns dark, its back entries, its black iron railings and Victorian schools with the words INFANTS and JUNIORS carved into stone. Because I moved away from it when I was only five, it stands there in the distance, still poorly mapped, a place of family stories and discreet silences, half-remembered things; lit by a few photographs with pinked edging, but essentially formless.

This is how many of us know our pasts. Watching *Distant Voices, Still Lives* again, I was freshly struck by its ways with time and memory, which it treats as an architectural thing, as building block and at the same time something fluid and musical. I was also led to wondering about home, or at least home as a place we first issue from, rather than the one that lies ahead of us. Upon telling people that I've been writing this little book about *Distant Voices, Still Lives*, I've also been struck by the number of times a face has lit up. The film might be set in Davies's childhood Liverpool, but it chimes with a multitude of post-war urban British upbringings; and while the particulars of this filmic family's lives might differ, something is widely recognised.

Writing at length on one film can feel a little like explaining a joke, or paraphrasing a poem. I hope this book, instead of offering a foreclosure on any individual viewing experience, sends the viewer back to look again for themselves at *Distant Voices, Still Lives*. Davies's film is nothing if it is not a reminder of what the projected motion picture can be: I hope I've accounted for the made-ness of the film, and the experience of watching it, rather than treating camerawork or soundtrack as surface symptoms of some huge central thesis the director wished to propound. I hold artistic intent in the highest respect, even though as a writer how could I *not* understand what Montale called the 'second life' of art?

As with many great poems, a précis of what actually happens in *Distant Voices, Still Lives* would not seem to amount to anything out of the ordinary: birth, marriage and death in a working-class Liverpool household of the 1940s and 1950s; the tension between a brutal, domineering father and a loving mother; the bond between these parents and their son and two daughters; the wider world of work and the pub, friends and going to the flicks. But the way in which these lives are revivified and photographed, unflinchingly but tenderly, and the way their ordinary, quotidian things and rituals are honoured and allowed their moment in the light, has transformed this small corner of Liverpool 5 into something resounding and majestic.

Rain

'Rain itself is something
Undoubtedly which happens in the past.'

Jorge Luis Borges, *La Lluvia*[3]

Distant Voices, Still Lives opens with a downpour. Before the picture fades up, even before the title has left the screen, we hear a peal of thunder, then rain, and then the BBC: 'The shipping forecast for today and tonight: Iceland, Bailey, Faroes …'. Out of the darkness emerges a terraced house with milk waiting on its step. It is teeming, the skies emptying, and the rain spatters into a haze above the short path and forms little spouts from ledges. A woman comes to the door and takes a long disapproving look at the foul weather as she kneels to bring in the three pints. '… Fair Isle,

Mother (Freda Dowie) bringing in the milk: the film's opening shot

Cromarty, Forties …' The camera is static, and the shot is tightly framed to the proportions of door, window and fence. We linger long enough, sitting in our darkness and dryness, to take it all in.

Rain in cinema seems to work in different ways: in *The Shawshank Redemption* (1994) it is the rinsing, redemptive element at the end of a tunnel; in films like *Stalker* (1979) or *Blade Runner* (1982) it provides a protean, light-catching dimension. In *Distant Voices, Still Lives* it seems to age the image with its vertical scrim and blurring. The BBC announcer's voice intoning the shipping forecast in RP reinforces this sense of the past, and we're also given a strange tang of the maritime, of vast Atlantic systems always 'moving in from the west'.

I absolutely adored it and I thought that's it, it's got to start with a mantra. And it's a strange but practical thing. We didn't know what it meant, we didn't realise these were areas in the sea, we just *didn't,* but you'd just sit there. I mean I didn't know what it meant, but it was extraordinarily magical. I thought if it starts with that, then it can go anywhere. You don't have to *say* 'this is memory': as soon as you hear that voice, you know it's time past. You *know*. It's like a dissolve.

The following shot takes us over the threshold with the woman, into a small hallway with a narrow flight of stairs to the left of centre, and the acoustic of the forecast shifts subtly to that of a radio indoors. We now realise this is a mother of three children by her intermittent calls upstairs to raise them: 'It's seven o'clock, you three!' The camera remains fixed upon the empty flight of stairs, but we hear the voices and footfall of the children coming down them. Each are greeted in turn out of shot. Eileen. Tony. Maisie. It is as if the image will come halfway to meet the viewer, but no more: on the other side of the screen, we have to imaginatively recreate and complete. With this most economical of openings we are given our bearings – the BBC announcer's accent, and perhaps the spartan hallway furnishings too, provides a rough guideline as to where we are in time; the shipping areas and the Liverpudlian accents of the children alert us to where we are in space – yet from the outset there's instability. The shipping forecast can be cosily reassuring heard at home, but we are unsure as to what kind of a passage we will have.

A dissolve with the power of a daydream: the hallway looking out onto Kensington Street

And then the camera does something extraordinary: we hear the opening of 'I Get the Blues When it's Raining' (sung unaccompanied by the actress Freda Dowie, who plays the mother) and it slowly begins to move forward into the hallway, swinging around to the right, tracking across the wall, then bringing the front door into view before coming to rest set at 180 degrees from where it started. The white noise of the rain increases again. It is as if we are inside a robot camera entering the spaces of a submerged wreck. An old black switch clings to the wall like a strange limpet.

It's a crucial scene also in the way it establishes – or doesn't establish – viewpoint. All of Davies's earlier films feature a clearly defined central character – Robert Tucker – who acts as a version of Davies himself, moving through childhood and schooldays (*Children*, 1976), then middle age (*Madonna and Child*, 1980) towards an imagined old age and death (*Death and Transfiguration*, 1983). But *Distant Voices, Still Lives*, while undoubtedly still drawing deeply on autobiography and offering a version of his childhood, doesn't feature a central character whom we can identify with Davies. This in fact is a central tenet of the film: instead of dramatising his memories and the anecdotal evidence of his family by characterising himself, Davies makes his film out of others' moments. And being in that hallway at the beginning, with the rain pouring down outside, feels like we're haunting a space, outside of time, looking in. The following dissolve, which makes the doorway open and the sunshine miraculously spill in, happens with all the imaginative power of a daydream.

It might appear, then, that Davies is something of a pluviophile. This rainy opening would seem to hold great emotional importance: it is as if a past is being recalled in which it is always raining, always a working day (every time I watch this opening, I'm convinced this is a Monday morning, even though there is no evidence of this on screen or in the script). The rainy emergence from the dark also reminds me of the 'Dark House' stanzas from Tennyson's *In Memoriam*:

> He is not here; but far away
>> The noise of life begins again,
>> And ghastly thro' the drizzling rain
> On the bald street breaks the blank day.[4]

Emotionally, a cloud is hung over the film: a threat of rain.

Much later on, in *Still Lives*, there is another rain-drenched sequence. It follows directly on from a walk back from the pub with Eileen and her husband Dave. They are living with Eileen's paternal grandmother, and Eileen is anxious they enter her house as quietly and as expeditiously as possible, though Dave is having none of it. He needs to take a piss against the wall – in the script, we are to hear *The sound of torrential pissing* – and sings as he does so: 'Up the lazy river, by the old mill run …'. In the script, this scene cuts to an interior at the grandmother's house, where Eileen and Dave are listening to the radio[5] – a scene that does survive, appearing earlier – but in the film Davies instead elides this banal, comic, almost squalid episode ('That lazy, lazy river, in the noonday sun …') with a huge pre-emptory shiver of strings, announcing a cut to the next scene.

We now see a canopy of umbrellas, lofted against heavy rain. As the camera begins to track upwards, we realise this is the queue outside a cinema: we see two posters – for *Love is a Many-Splendored Thing*, whose theme tune we begin to realise we are hearing, and a coming attraction, *Guys and Dolls*, which, if we count the pop-cultural tree rings, means this is 1955 – and, above the gothic-arched poster boards, signs for the Futurist (a cinema in Lime Street, long closed down now). The camera keeps tracking upwards, past two downcast spot-lamps that are also illuminating the deluge within their beams, and we dissolve out of the rain, with a shimmer of strings, into the cinema interior. By now, we realise the music is calling the shots. Inside, the general lift continues, as the camera continues to crane upwards across rows of people watching a movie that we don't actually ever see: a back-light – the projector, perhaps – picks out scuds of blue cigarette smoke. It finally comes to rest in a medium close-up of sisters Eileen and Maisie. They are both in floods of tears.

This gorgeous, lyrical sequence isn't over yet. I should pause though, and wonder how this image, of the two sisters crying in the cinema dark, is this sequence's still centre: time having caught up with itself. It's as if the first throb of music, heard at the very close of the scene outside the grandmother's house, has finally locked into its lush, melodramatic moment: two viewers being exposed to the full force of cinema. *Distant Voices, Still Lives* is full of such slippages between image and voiceover or soundtrack, full of movements around events rather than narrative progressions. Davies has written of how the film 'constantly turns back on itself, like the ripples in a pool when a stone is thrown into it'.[6]

There is then an abrupt cut – with a corresponding shift in tempo from the music – to what I first took to be an image on screen, a large white abstract diptych. After a moment, two figures fall slowly into view and your sense of the picture plane needs to make a huge readjustment. They hit what you realise is distempered glass with a low echoing boom and, again, an orchestral counterpoint of vibes left hanging in the air. They disappear from view in a hail of dancing shards: a screen shattering into thousands of pieces. (In the script, George and Tony come crashing through a glass roof we are *looking up* at.) We cut to a door being noisily swung open, and the music abruptly ceases, as Maisie runs through the rain to be at her husband George's hospital bedside. We come to realise that Tony and his brother-in-law have fallen off their scaffolding in a bad accident at work.

The accident scene demonstrates another defining feature of Davies's technique in *Distant Voices, Still Lives*, which extends his method of building the film from a mixture of others' moments and his own memory. Davies's brother and brother-in-law did indeed suffer bad accidents, but not both at the same time:

Those were two separate accidents. But dramatically, two separate accidents are not interesting. They're not. My brother-in-law George was a builder, he fell off some scaffolding, and got £2,500 compensation. Which was an enormous sum of money in those days. And my brother was in the army, and some ammunition boxes fell on him and broke his leg. But I wanted both accidents to happen at the same time, which isn't literally true. But it should be something that is strange, because I wasn't there when he fell off the scaffolding, and I wasn't in the army. When I used to go to Liverpool, I don't think it's there any more, but just on the left-hand side, after Woolton, there used to be a laundry? Was it the Lune Laundry? With those glass roofs. And I thought: 'What if they fall through glass?' And that's how it came about.

It's as if memories heard second-hand as family stories, and childhood memories themselves, are malleable, and can be edited together and organised formally. Reality is rearranged to achieve a formal truth. The poet Michael Donaghy once spoke to me about this fugitive aspect of 'true', a word that can mean fidelity to what actually happened, but also, as a verb, mean to adjust so as to *make* true.[7]

The whole movement is like a parabola. There is a gradual sense of take-off and lift in the expectant queue of umbrellas outside the Futurist; there is the extended high of being immersed in a movie; there is a violent falling back to earth. The sequence ends up in hospital – all cream ceramic tiling and metal bedsteads: you can almost smell the institutional disinfectant and stale milk – at the bedsides of George, then Tony. At first we see Maisie keeping her vigil next to George ('We fell off the bleeding scaffolding, May …') and then, instead of a cut to another bedside, Davies does something unusual with the camera again; in many ways as similarly strange as when we entered the hallway at the beginning of the film. To the sound of Tommy Riley playing 'Galway Bay' on the harmonica (Anthony Burgess's 'sad instrument of the Somme'), we crane up and around to a hospital window, where the camera holds for a few moments, before craning backwards to its original position: except this time we are at Tony's bedside. There is no obvious edit or dissolve. The camera movement is there in the screenplay – Davies always embarks upon shooting with a clear, definite idea of every shot, set-up and accompanying soundtrack from the script, though the script is put aside once the first assemblies have been made – and it's an oddly affecting device: another slippage and suspension of time, employing the simplest of means. As the camera holds on the hospital window, before we begin the crane back into the ward, there's time to look outside through one of the film's many frames-within-frames. It is wire-strengthened, institutional glass, and beyond it, as it has been all along, it is pouring with rain.

House

'And build an edifice of form
For a house where phantoms may keep warm.'

William Empson, *This Last Pain*[8]

From the outset, the Davies's modest terraced house is a character in itself. It is the childhood home, the centre of the universe. Davies had already made a version of it – in his first film, *Children*, the co-ordinates of hallway and parlour and fireside and bedroom are already starting to be mapped out – but by the time he made *Distant Voices, Still Lives*, its spaces are shown and explored by the camera to a much more convincing and striking effect. Shooting on location wasn't an option, for a number of reasons:

That house where I grew up was demolished in '61. And it was unique ... I was able to rebuild it for *The Long Day Closes*, but we didn't have a huge budget for *Distant Voices, Still Lives*, so we had to find something that looked ... working class. A working-class street, and we shot in Drayton Park, but there were no cellars, so it wasn't like our house ... We had to go with what was there, because we didn't have the money. So that was a practical thing.

From the opening face-on shot of the house's façade in the rain, the camera seems poised or led, in so many of its framing and tracking shots, by doorways, windows, hallways and house-fronts.[9] You can't watch the film and not on some level imaginatively inhabit these spaces.

I have to admit to the personal appeal of seeing such a house re-created and explored so intimately. My family lived in a succession of houses similar to it, the last being near Edge Hill at the end of the 1960s. And it's this house I can just remember – the 'old house' – before the area was cleared for demolition and we were rehoused in Netherley, a new estate a few miles away (the first time I spoke to Davies on the phone, he told me he remembered this being built). This new housing – some of it

Maisie: 'Can I go to the dance, Dad?'

still unfinished – was exciting and echoey, and smelled of cut wood and wet cement, and there were insects and birds I hadn't seen before, because Netherley was built on the very edge of Liverpool, where rural Lancashire began. But I missed the old house and street, and its spaces seemed to sink in. I looked forward to visits to relatives who hadn't been moved. I missed what I can only describe as the mystery of age and texture: in a somewhat larger sense, Eva Hoffman writes of a similar sense of change between the rich textures of an old-world city (Krakow in Poland), and the blanker, thinner spaces of Vancouver.[10] My parents, sick of outside lavatories and house mice, were understandably relieved.

But this house built out of film has a wider veracity. It's just so clearly defined. Early on in the film, we see Maisie having to scrub the cellar floor before she can go out to a dance. ('But Dad, there's rats down there – I'm terrified of rats.' 'No cellar – no dance!') Later, we see the family in the cellar years earlier, chopping wood and bundling it under the watchful eye of the father. Contrast this with the higher rooms of the house, where we see the mother sat on a ledge cleaning the sun-struck window; or, the bedroom, airy with billowing curtains and flooded with light while the mother talks in voiceover ('I love the light nights …'). In between, the hallway and parlour are the scenes of so many comings and goings and gatherings.

All of this constructs a strong sense of verticality. Even though *Distant Voices, Still Lives* temporally turns back on itself and moves fluidly across time and space, it is always adding to and reinforcing this sense of a dwelling place. And because it has this sense of verticality, it easily chimes with a deep sense of domestic space many of us still have. It chimes with

'I love the light nights ...'

phenomenology and Gaston Bachelard's cellar as irrational place, as the dark entity of the house; the nooks and havens of corners; the house's different levels and spaces as repositories for memories and daydreaming.[11]

W. H. Auden too was interested in 'the geography of the house', and in *About the House* cellars and attics are similarly mapped; and though Auden's poems posit a slightly different relationship between mothers and fathers and domestic spaces, some lines strikingly support Davies's screen house:

> Encrust with years of clammy grime, the lair, maybe,
> Of creepy-crawlies or a ghost, its flag-stoned vault
> Is not for girls ...[12]

It also chimes with Carl Jung's model of psychic structure, from the ancient cellar and Neolithic cave to the upper storey of the 19th century.[13] And it chimes with some deep-rooted understanding of a house as a living, breathing entity. So when Alec Guinness, in *The Ladykillers*, explains how 'I always thought windows were the eyes of a house ... Didn't someone say the eyes are the windows of the soul?' we know right away what he means. The corpulence of bricks and mortar: when Rainer Maria Rilke finally finished his *Duino Elegies*, he praised the site of completion thus: 'I went outside into the cold moonlight and stroked little Muzot [a chateau] like a big animal, its old walls which granted this to me ...'[14]

Also, as in *The Ladykillers*, so much takes place in the hallway, with its staircase and newel-post prominent in so many shots. Apart from that beautifully atmospheric Ealing space – a chamber still filled with the

barometer-tapping details of the *belle époque* in 1950s London[15] – another hallway that comes to mind appears in David Lean's *This Happy Breed* (1944), where the family, leaving their house (and the film) for the final time, close the door and the empty hallway floods with absence. And perhaps *Performance* (1970): that ominous shot of James Fox having just crossed the threshold of 81 Powis Square. There's also something of the boxy, rectilinear stairwells that are found in the films of Nicholas Ray. Stairs seem to play an important role in all of Davies's films: from the escape route of the child to the sanctuary of his bedroom in *Children*; and Robert's painful, one-foot-in-front-of-another progress down them, careful not to wake his mother, in *Madonna and Child*; to the scene of the murder in *The Neon Bible* and the magnificent silver balustrade of Manderston House in *The House of Mirth*. The newel-post I will return to.

I loved it. We had *nothing*, it was falling to bits, but I truly loved it because after my father died we really were happy there. From 7 till 11 I was in a permanent state of ecstasy. Permanent ecstasy. So yes, very often I was in the house on my own. I'd wait for them to come back, just sit and wait, that's what I did. So I knew that house … it was like another family member.

The hallway and newel-post in *The Ladykillers* (1955)

Thresholds

In many ways, all of the fixtures and fittings in Davies's autobiographical films – and, to a degree, those he has made later – are repeated attempts at re-creating the spaces of a childhood. *Distant Voices, Still Lives* and *The Long Day Closes* in particular are a kind of testament to just how little can be required – a fanlight in summer, a radio downstairs, the sun coming out on carpet – to sustain a child's imaginative growth. The recurrence of not just stairs and halls, but other domestic spaces and things in his films reminds me of a number of artists who have returned again and again to some scene or object that is endlessly significant to them. The purpose isn't necessarily progression, but a kind of circulation. In the same way Pierre Bonnard was drawn to 'the same pots, carafes, chairs, vases, the same blue cigarette box, the same oval wicker basket, the same interiors …'[16] so Davies can be said to be compelled by his childhood home's early arrangement of things, its shadows, the way light fell during certain hours of the day.

What I think that house meant, and my family … I thought there was nothing like that or them in the world. I really did think that. It was special. I don't know why, I just remember feeling ecstatically happy about it. But people did spend a lot of time on the doorstep, or looking through windows. The pace of life was very different; you made your own entertainment a lot of the time.

With a strong sense of its terraced house,[17] *Distant Voices, Still Lives* also looks out into the larger world. The film is full of thresholds, most notably that between hallway and street. In one memorable scene, we see Doreen Mather, who has come to mind Maisie's baby, paused before the open doorway, gazing into the hallway. Neither inside nor out, she's singing from 'Dreamboat' softly to herself on the step, and slowly turning through a full circle (echoing the camera movement in the opening empty hallway scene). This is the era of doors being left open. The insurance man Mr Spaull appears at the same threshold, parties spill over it, and a young Tony is barred from crossing it by his father:

So you were in the house, you were in the street, and that peculiar relationship between what is private and what is public is very, very odd.

Because your house was your absolute inner sanctum, although people
were always welcome, and people came, but it was yours, even though we
only rented it. Sitting on the step was that halfway thing of having your house
behind you and there was the world. And that peculiar thing of being in the
street and looking at the house and not seeing it as just one of a terrace ...

The pub, hospital, church and cinema are all visited in turn, but this is
mostly a world of interiors. Within what has to be considered a tiny budget
(the two films in total cost £750,000), the film is a small miracle of period
look and accuracy. The superstructure of the house is stocked with detail.
At the same time as Davies is a great admirer of the Hollywood musical,
with its hermetically sealed sense of design and artifice, he is also a stickler
for period detail: 'That's what angers me about things set in the 1950s,
because they always get it wrong.' He understands styles and periods do
not end neatly upon strokes of midnight as if by decree, and that times
overlap. So, in a similar way, the primary school I went to was much, much
closer to the 1950s than it is to today, this world of interiors he grew up in
was furnished with things already decades old by mid-century. Speaking of
The House of Mirth:

I know what those kind of stifling interiors are like – I remember going into
houses that were still Victorian, so circumscribed, we can't imagine now
what it was like. The fact that someone in authority, even when I was growing
up, would say [snaps fingers], 'Don't do that!' – and you stopped. It
materially alters what you look at and how you feel. But I do love that
enclosed world.[18]

Distant Voices, Still Lives re-creates the world of surfaces before Lincrusta
and Artex, before knotty-pine wallpaper and frosted bubble glass. As our
parents took to this home DIY palette in the 1970s in our newbuild
housing, they also noticed there were no fireplaces – all of the houses were
centrally heated – so almost everybody I knew employed a bricklayer to
build a fake fireplace surround, with artificial, bulb-lit plastic coals at its
centre. The old, darkwood furniture people had brought with them didn't
sit right in these new boxy spaces, and I remember bonfires of wardrobes

and chests of drawers and ottomans. *Distant Voices*, especially, features the fire at the centre of the house – literally the Latin *focus* – and reminds us of the domestic hearth's last stand as focal point before television became the centre of attention. (The Davies household didn't own a television set until 1960.)

In *Distant Voices, Still Lives* I sense a world restored, and restored lovingly. The entire film is an act of ecopoesis.[19] There is a difference, though, in weight of detail between the distressed bare surfaces of *Distant Voices*, where the father is very much the central presence, and *Still Lives*, which is a kind of aftermath: the *mise en scène* becomes lusher, busier, more detailed. After the bare wallpapered rooms of *Distant Voices*, we start to see an accretion of things on mantelpieces, the texture of Bakelite and bric-a-brac, even fronds and ornament (look at the background, for instance, when Tony is listening to the radio or checking his coupon; or when Maisie is singing to her baby). It's as if a bleaker, harder-edged space has been softened with a slow coral growth of love and carefree inattention.

The pulse and shape of the interior of this house have an aural counterpoint (as well as that of music). Often the world of the street outside can be heard, but for an era when the street was a place heavily populated by children at play (a view reinforced by the contemporaneous street photographs of Roger Mayne in North Kensington, or, closer to home, Harry Ainslough in Liverpool) we see little of the games, or walls chalked with goalposts, or back entries, or dogs.[20] Through some of the film's many thresholds we are sometimes aware of it, and the wild sound is as 'authentic' as that from one of Scorsese's New York apartments (especially *Taxi Driver* [1976] and *Raging Bull* [1980]), but the camera rarely ventures forth down these streets. Vehicles draw up or pull away slowly – the hearse at the film's opening, Eileen's taxi departure for Phwelli, and subsequent return; Tony's marriage at the close of the film – but this is a world of interiors.

That the camera dwells in the spaces of this house so much must owe a great deal to Davies's childhood perception of space. When he speaks of his childhood in Kensington Street, you begin to understand his sensitivity to space, engendered by long solitary hours, often waiting for family members to come home. There was no television in this household throughout the 1950s, no shelves filled with books. You also begin to understand how there were two spaces nested over time within one house: those created while Davies's father was still alive:

I'm still acutely aware of atmosphere in a room. When I was a kid I'd run into a room and if he didn't want anyone around, he'd just kick me from one end of the house to the other. You don't make that mistake very often.[21]

And those created in his aftermath:

And that house was a magnet, an absolute magnet, and it grew because it had my mother's love in it. It's odd, because the daughter who takes most after my mother, Maisie, her house is the same, it draws people. Some houses do.

Family

'Art is a house that tries to be haunted.'

Emily Dickinson[22]

Births. Deaths. Marriages. The great cycle of life, as refracted through the absolutely ordinary, could be described as the central project of *Distant Voices, Still Lives*, and the film's circular structures radiate out from these events. The family constantly renewing itself has to entail an ongoing breaking apart: while the film is capacious enough to be conscious of the former, anxieties about the latter seem to have fuelled much of Davies's work, and its ideas of what 'home' means:

And dread comes over me as the house echoes in the dark, as Fridays become as cold as Sundays … And mother and I are left utterly alone. The house rattles and calls, the house with its rich, its voluptuous memories, crumbles into disrepair as the rats gnaw in the cellar and the distemper in the bare, empty rooms cracks.[23]

The film's first dissolve – of the front door, seen from inside the hallway on a rainy morning, opening onto sunlight – leads us straight from the heart of one of these themes into the centre of another. Slowly, a hearse pulls up outside the front door, its coffin cargo slotting into frame and standstill: one of Seamus Heaney's 'black glaciers'.[24] There is then a dissolve from this hallway into a sequence book-ended with probably the most discussed and analysed images in the film (and emblematic: these 'family portraits' were used as its stills and publicity materials). We move into the parlour, where the family have gathered – Eileen, Tony, Maisie, and their mother, seated – dressed for the funeral. They stand stock still: the shot is held like this for a few moments, before the camera begins a slow zoom into the group, towards a black-and-white photograph on the otherwise bare parlour wall behind them. Quite suddenly, starting with the mother, they each peel away out of shot, leaving the camera moving closer into the photograph, which we can see is of a man holding on to a horse: given the context, this must be the mourned father.

It's always incredibly arresting simply because of the plane of attention: the family are lined up, looking back straight at the viewer (apart from the mother: her gaze is downcast). And it's always a slight shock when they break rank, simply because they had been standing so still, as if held by the impedimenta of head-holders or knee-braces for a

Stasis and movement 1:
the family gathered for
the father's funeral

slow exposure. A part of me always mischievously looks for the slightest tic or sway of body weight that will betray the effect when I watch the film now; the same impulse that arises in the frozen table-tennis scene during Powell and Pressburger's *A Matter of Life and Death* (1946), though there's a big difference I think between the former and latter scenes in terms of directorial intent. This shot has also latterly reminded me of those early documentary films, popularised in 2005 by the television series *The Lost World of Mitchell and Kenyon*, where film-makers cannily took pictures outside factories or on football terraces in the knowledge that their subjects would often pay to see themselves later on screen. Many of these people had yet to grow accustomed to moving imagery, and often hold themselves or strike a pose, then walk out of shot: cinema caught in the act of replacing still photography.

The photograph of the father hangs behind glass on a chain. We now dissolve back to the hallway, then the waiting hearse, following the family out, framed by the shapes of the house, and seen from inside then outside. Then we dissolve from the empty hallway back into the parlour, and the same family group faces us again. Except this time they are dressed for Eileen's wedding. Again, there is a slow zoom into the group, this time holding on Eileen and her brother Tony. They are framed so that the photograph of their father hangs between them in the background. The effect is of a circle being drawn. The entire sequence is underwritten and bound together by what's happening on the soundtrack: not a word of dialogue is spoken, but we have been listening to Jessye Norman singing 'There's a Man Goin' Round Takin' Names' the whole time.

Tony (Dean Williams) on Eileen's wedding day, thinking of his father

Maisie: 'He was a bastard, and I bleedin' hated him'

At the precise moment the song ends – another feat of choreography – Eileen turns to Tony and says: 'I wish me Dad was here.' He looks towards her, and then we pan to the right, and Maisie, who is maintaining a look of normal service, but thinking in voiceover: 'I don't. He was a bastard, and I bleedin' hated him.' In the first five minutes, we have learned a great deal about this family:

After coming back from America with the *Trilogy*, the BFI commissioned me to do a feature and that had been in the back of my mind for a long time and so that's what I wanted to do. But I couldn't cope with the writing of ten people; I just wasn't experienced enough … It had been around in my mind for a long time exactly because I wanted to try and chart that suffering. Not because it changes anything – it doesn't – but when they said we'd like to commission, that was it. And then I sat down to write the screenplay, I think for over a year, just letting my memories come back to me, and I wrote them down. It took about ten months or so. It coalesced more or less into a story.

This family on screen represent a distillation of Davies's own family. He discovered early on that he could write something based around their experiences by limiting the central characters to his mother, father and three siblings. Again, this is a trueing of actual events.

To achieve this distillation, Davies drew upon something of a family of specialists, many of whom he had already worked with: Bill Diver, the film's cinematographer and editor, had shot all of Davies's films since

Stasis and
movement 2: father
(Pete Postlethwaite)
erupts at the
Christmas dinner
table

Children in 1976; the film's producer, Jennifer Howarth, had studied with Davies at the National Film School; art director Miki van Zwanenberg had worked on *Death and Transfiguration*. This was Davies's first film to credit a costume designer, Monica Howe, with whom he has worked on every film since: 'a costume designer of genius'.[25] There is then a sense of teamwork and collaboration, though the director's central vision, as he acknowledges himself, is always paramount.

Davies was the youngest of ten children, the baby boomer, born in a working-class Catholic household in post-war Liverpool. His father died when he was six-and-a-half, though the memories of him as a powerful, domineering, violent man are vivid and, together with the love and support of his mother, form a huge tension in *Distant Voices, Still Lives*. (And his next film, *The Long Day Closes*, with Bud's cellar nightmare, takes place entirely in the aftermath of his father's death.) Looking at all of Davies's autobiographical films, which interpenetrate and overlap to an extraordinary degree, it's possible to discern many elements of this tension, though other undercurrents are always present. So in his *Trilogy*, *Children* contains some harrowing scenes of the father's illness (Davies's father was ill with cancer for two years) and proclivity for violence, but also the terrors of school, and the first stirrings of sexuality. *Madonna and Child* brings the latter aspect to the fore, and explores the dangers and sheer frustrating awkwardness of being gay and working class and Catholic in 1960s Liverpool. *Distant Voices, Still Lives* differs, as I've mentioned, by not really having a central character we can identify with Terence Davies. In this way, it's a film with a hole in it. And it's also a film about what happens when the centre – in this case, a brutal patriarch – doesn't hold. The whole film shows a family as if caught in a whirlpool.

The cast he assembled ranged from those who were relatively experienced in front of the camera by that point – Freda Dowie (who played Mother) would have been familiar to many viewers from much television work in the 1960s and 1970s – to Dean Williams (Tony), who had appeared in hardly anything, but who has so much to do (and does it brilliantly) in the film. Though not quite Bressonian – I've never heard Davies refer to his cast as 'models' – there is still a sense of by and large avoiding 'names', preferring instead the right voice, face and presence.

(This is borne out by an anecdote to be found among *The House of Mirth*'s Extra Features on DVD: Davies was keen to cast, in the lead role of Lily Bart, an actress whose face brought to mind a *fin de siècle*, John Singer Sergeant 'look': he came upon a publicity still of Gillian Anderson. When informed of her worldwide fame via *The X Files*, Davies confessed he'd never heard of such a thing, and that he only attributed paranormal powers to the Inland Revenue.) Pete Postlethwaite (Father) has since gone on to great screen success, appearing in everything from *The Usual Suspects* (1995) to *The Constant Gardener* (2005). Both he and Michael Starke (Dave) – who was soon to become better known as Sinbad in the soap opera *Brookside* – like others in the cast had their roots in theatre: Liverpool has nurtured a galaxy of stage actors between its Playhouse and Everyman. Lorraine Ashbourne and Angela Walsh are both stunning as sisters Maisie and Eileen. A young Pauline Quirke appears briefly as Doreen. Andrew Schofield, who has a small part playing Jingles's nemesis Les, would have been familiar as television's 'Scully' in Liverpool and beyond, and had recently hit the big screen playing Johnny Rotten in Alex Cox's *Sid and Nancy* (1986).

Postlethwaite's father manages to cast quite a pall over *Distant Voices*. We hear his voice – full of attack, its default setting seemingly the barking of orders – before we actually see him (though the photograph on the parlour wall in the funeral and wedding gatherings is an *actual* photograph of Davies's father). Our first shot of him – during the cellar scene as Maisie scrubs the stone floor – is from the waist down: dark slacks and shiny shoes, followed by an eruption of violence. He is the voice of the house ordering Eileen to get inside as she and Micky linger on the step for one last ciggie after the dance. (Much later on in the film, in *Still Lives*, we hear the grandmother's – *his* mother's – voice in a similar role: Eileen waking the paternal dead.) When the family goes to visit him in hospital, it's his voice itself that seems stricken, thwarted: his agonised 'I was wrong, son' to Tony is strangulated, gurgled, bent out of shape.

He is so often an aggressor, either physical or frozen mute. In the frosty Christmas dinner scene he moves from one state to the other before our very eyes, and it is heartbreaking. All the family, except the mother, are present and waiting: he sits at the head of the small table. On the foremost of all the annual holidays and high days, at what should be the prime family gathering of the year, Postlethwaite's hands begin to shake, and soon his entire body seems racked by some invisible force he is struggling to, but can't, contain. (Robert Louis Stevenson would have described this as 'a picnic on a volcano'.) In the end the tablecloth is yanked away, and all the food and crockery along with it, and he yells for his wife to 'clean it up!'. Later, at the other end of *Distant Voices*, he has turned back into a voice again, a shade: as the camera moves through an upstairs room flooded with light, with curtains billowing, we hear him calling her name, aggressively, as thunder rumbles.

A more clement aspect of *Distant Voices, Still Lives* – and one likely to command the assent of any viewer from a remotely similar background – is just how socially accurate the portrayal of this family is, out into its extended parts. We see Eileen and her husband Dave domiciled with her paternal grandmother, a reminder of the British housing shortage of the post-war years. The phrase 'disposable income' waits in the future. We might have forgotten, but for a long time it was not at all unusual to find newly married couples co-habiting with their parents and new in-laws. Asking around discloses how recently this state of affairs was the status quo: my parents both lived with my grandparents when they were first married; my wife's parents lived above her grandparents' pub in a similar

situation. The effect of circumscribing newlyweds in this way, in houses that were usually small and spaces that were far from private, often created its own enormous tensions and a social dynamic difficult to appreciate from an early twenty-first-century vantage point.

Even though she is only in a few scenes, this grandmother seems to plug the film into something superstitious, folkloric, even downright uncanny. Midway through *Distant Voices*, we see Eileen, Tony and Maisie as children, in the dark, lit by a candle. We realise this is a mirror, just as her old face looms into view: 'If you look into a mirror at midnight – you'll see the devil.' She also has something to do with a funny but unsettling scene later on in *Still Lives*: Eileen and Dave, newly married and living under her roof, are listening to the radio while eating their tea, when Uncle Ted – Eileen's paternal uncle – puts his face around the door, and switches off the light. He is holding a candle on a saucer, so his face becomes lit from below as he says, in a weird singsong voice: 'I've switched the light off – I don't know whether I'm doing right or wrong-a.'

Uncle Ted 'acting soft'

It's a completely unsettling irruption, but also a perfect personification of the essential alienness of entering into, and being suddenly part of, a new family: 'Who the bleedin' hell was that?' asks a rattled Dave.

That's what he used to do. I was terrified of him. Do you know a song called 'Some of These Days'? 'Some of these days you're gonna miss me ...'. And he'd sing it with this kind of psychotic aggression. [Laughter] He'd go: 'Some ... of these ... days ... you're gonna *miss* me ...'. Absolutely terrifying. Nutters, the crowd of them. The bloke who played him, Carl [Chase], had a small role in one of the *Batman* films, and they were rehearsing this night scene, lots of people, and Jack Nicholson, who played The Joker ... They had a break, and he said he was walking across the set, and Jack Nicholson came up and said: 'You were Uncle Ted, weren't you.' Isn't that amazing?

Much of *Still Lives* seems to revolve around the drawn-out christening celebrations for Maisie's baby, with her family and friends all wetting the baby's head in a series of sing-alongs at the local pub. Births mark another point of separation from the family, as the new mothers and fathers adjust and realign their lives around the central pulse of their babies. This part of the film is shot through with a sense of the family breaking up into smaller units; the old gang meet occasionally in the pub (nicely echoed in song at one point by 'Back in the Old Routine') but the triumvirate of Eileen, Micky and Jingles – who once sat around a table in awe of a bottle of

Micky, Eileen and Jingles: Chanel No.5 from a 'Cunard Yank'

Chanel No.5 – is losing its corners. Back indoors, in *Distant Voices*, we hear Dave exercising dominion over Eileen:

> DAVE: (*Voiceover*) You're married now – I'm your husband – your duty's to me, frig everyone else. Monica, Jingles, that's all ancient history now.

These women are learning that they must tread carefully in their new roles. Old pals aren't always welcomed by their spouses: Les (a Brylcreemed martinet) won't even cross the pub to say hello to Jingles's former gang. Even their sense of geography seems to have shifted:

> MONICA: … So don't be a stranger – otherwise I'll not see you till next Preston Guild. We're only in Jubilee Drive – you're only ten minutes away.
> EILEEN: (*Half-hearted*) We'll see … I'll try and come round.
> MONICA: Or I could come over to yours. You're only in Vane Street, aren't you?
> EILEEN: Oh you'd better not, Micky, he's funny about having visitors.

At such points, there's a terrible sense of circularity in the film: are we seeing a version of their parents' union, repeatedly played out? For the girls who pitched their tent together on Formby Sands, this is the end of their togetherness.

In the film as a whole, the actual birth occupies a very central position. In the screenplay, it comes at the very beginning of *Still Lives* – the two pieces are clearly separated as written pieces – just following on from a simple title. But on screen, the birth scene works as a kind of bridge, the connective tissue, between the two halves of the film, and helps unite the whole.

> EXT. NIGHT
> *Close-up of water. River Mersey, dark and rippling. Rain.*

The passage is so much more compelling because of the tindery-ness that immediately precedes it. The mother is alone asleep in the parlour, which is licked by a warm firelight. The paper slides from her lap. The camera

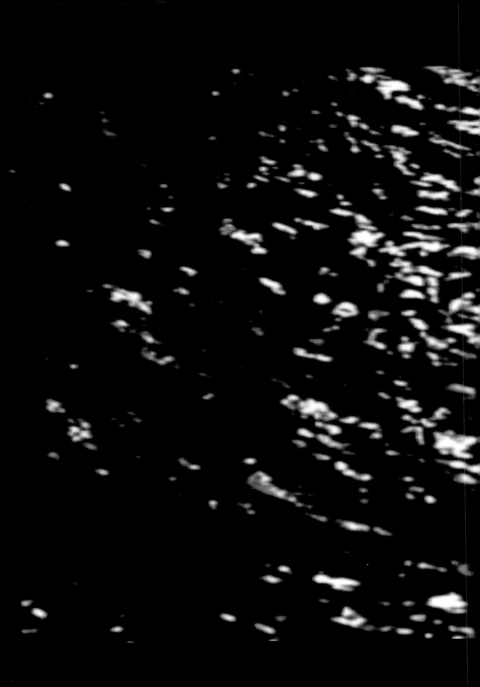

tracks in on the crackling fire itself, slowly, and then fades to black. In the darkness, to the right of screen, there are small sparks of light, and we slowly realise we are looking at dark water. We hear a choir – they are singing Benjamin Britten's 'A Hymn to the Virgin' – as light now picks up more of the rippling waveforms, and we hear the screams and howls of labour. The dark water dissolves into the birth room at Mill Road, and the camera tracks alongside Maisie, her hand clutching the bed rail. (This camera moving across the face of the waters also foreshadows the scene in *The House of Mirth*, where the Atlantic off New England is elided into the Mediterranean.)

This watery crossing opens up something vast and elemental within the diurnal. It also gives the film a strange corporeality (in the same way the film's house is characterised, is a living, breathing thing). Once the simple title for *Still Lives* appears, we are listening to *Two-Way Family Favourites* coming from somewhere inside the house, while the baby is sunning in the pram. Despite the avoidance of conventional narrative and any strict chronology, the film does create its own internal logic, beginning with a BBC shipping forecast aubade, and ending with the lights-out of last orders and the late walk home from the marriage party. And entering into the lazy long afternoon, *Still Lives*, with its baby on the step, Dickie Valentine crooning on the radio, new father George dozing in an armchair and Tony at rest, checking his coupons or listening to the racing (featuring a horse called *Come to Daddy*), reinforces the sense of the film having its own circadian rhythms.

Besides being important to film-making – and Davies has managed to budget all of his films remarkably well, perhaps a legacy of his days working as a book-keeper, which, by his own account, he was good at – money is shown to be important to this family. The father is often seen to hold the purse strings in *Distant Voices*: see how he throws some loose change to clatter contemptuously onto the cellar floor when Maisie asks to go to the dance; then tosses a coin sweetly for Micky – who can always charm and 'get round' Mr D. – to catch, when the girls, again, want to go out dancing. After Tony comes home AWOL and punches out the windows ('Come out and fight me, ya bastard!'), he attempts a reconciliation with his father by the fireside. (Look at that bloody hand

George and Tony in the long afternoon of the Macmillan government

clutching the bottles of Double Diamond!) When he icily refuses to have a drink with his son, Tony throws what little change he has into the fire: 'Tuppence. That's all I've got. But I wouldn't give *you* daylight.'

Money matters to these people, in the way it always matters to people who haven't got any. Later, we see the dead father laid out with pennies on his eyes: change for the ferryman. In *Still Lives*, there is quite an extended sequence showing the insurance man, Mr Spaull, from the Royal Liver, who pulls up on his bike and is accepted over the Davies's threshold like a member of the family (which in many ways he was: Davies remembers the sadness in the household on news of his retirement). This could be the only motion picture to mention a tontine, or paying the Club Man. In *The House of Mirth*, Lily Bart will find out, painfully, just how easy it always is for some people to fall onto life's rubbish heap.

Voices

'It's worse than Alcatraz, isn't it?'

Eileen

There is a great, unwritten oral culture, some of which survives in myth and tale and parable. A great deal, however, goes by the board. It would be sweeping and erroneous to suggest that the urban working classes of the post-war period were all great talkers and tellers of their own particular fables; but it feels that way to me, and the decline of talk is lamentable. *Distant Voices, Still Lives* owes its very shape and existence to stories:

After my father died in '52, the family talked all the time; it was their way of getting therapy. They were coming to terms with how badly he'd treated them. Because he was psychotic, infinitely worse than what's seen in the film, believe me: that's *nothing* to what he was like. And so I imbibed these memories as a child; that's where they were put into my mind, and because my family told stories so vividly, they became sort of my memories.

This could also account for the attraction many of us feel towards the world we are born into. Not only do we have the very edges of childhood memory, but there is also that mysterious region where private and collective memory intersect.[26] This is a pliant zone for any artist to be working in. The 'trueings' I spoke of earlier must become more viable, and a respect for the shape of remembered things – which are anything but linear and chronological – and the emotional weight accorded them, can prevail.

The film extends from wartime – the city of Liverpool, second port of Empire and HQ of the Western Approaches, was heavily bombed during the early years of the war: in one scene we see the family taking underground shelter from a bad raid – all the way to the cusp of the 1960s, and the high noon of the Macmillan government, when Davies would have been fifteen years old and leaving school to go to work. So there's a spectrum of available and adopted memory, if you like: pre-birth all the way through to late adolescence. The importance of storytelling within the family becomes apparent.

Within my own family, the war and its aftermath were often spoken of when I was very young. In fact, my childhood felt (and temporally was) very close to the 1950s and early 1960s, and this must constitute at least part of my fascination with *Distant Voices, Still Lives*. Such interpenetration can retain a powerful hold over us. I can easily remember my parents talking of air raids when they were children, and the terrible bombing of Clint Road shelter (I attended infants school there at the end of the 1960s) in great detail: scores irretrievably buried; the site filled in with quicklime. My mother, a child in Scourfield Street, took shelter in her aunt's cellar: all the houses on one side of the street had them. She would cross the Clint Road bombsite on her way to Brae Street School, and collect bright pieces of ceramic tiling winkled out of the mosaic floors. A story concerning two aunts of mine who died as babies was told to me so many times I feel as if I can picture the room where they were laid out.

And the culture puts voices in our ears, too. Sometimes, after asking us, as children, to do something, my mother would add the strange suffix: 'Funf has spoken.' It wasn't until recently I realised she was using a catchphrase from 1940s radio! In the same way, my father's speech was peppered with 'finks' and 'dames', words that had crossed the Atlantic on celluloid, as well as the idiom of the city. Things were always 'worse than Alcatraz' or 'like Fort Knox'. In the film, Jingles appears out of the dark at Eileen's wedding singing Gershwin's ''Swonderful!', which is immediately picked up by Eileen and Micky; then all three launch into their version of 'Too Young': 'They tried to sell us egg foo yung!'

Even in America. I remember when it was first showing there, there's a group of women who run the Film Archive, and one of them, Joanne Koch her name was, lovely lady; when the three of them get together and sing: 'They tried to sell us egg foo yung', she said: 'We used to sing that.' All those thousands of miles away, and they used to sing it.

Another undeniable attraction for me is the veracity of the voices in *Distant Voices, Still Lives*. Davies assembled a cast of mainly (up until then) little-known actors and actresses, and drew upon many native Liverpudlian speakers. This means that place in the film is geographically specific and widely identifiable even beyond these shores, without any recourse to landmarks or civic symbols:

The accent was much broader. My sisters didn't have one but my brothers did … 'can't' was 'kaahhnt'. So it was a much broader accent. But at the time of *Distant Voices, Still Lives* there was received pronunciation, and everything you heard on the radio was received pronunciation. I remember going to the sound archive on Great Portland Street, and getting these recordings out, just for *Two-Way Family Favourites* … That went out every Sunday from twelve o'clock to half-past one. And I heard this recording. At the time you didn't think anything, it was Jean Metcalfe, but then you hear [adopts cut-glass accent]: 'This is *Two-Way Family Favourites*. Hello everyone.' You can't believe it! That's the way they talked. You hear them and you just think: God. We never thought they sounded so far back. We just thought they were posh, and if they were posh they were infinitely superior, and you had to obey them, because they knew better. They were well bred.

This could be the same 'absolute speaker' a young Seamus Heaney was listening to across the water in 1940s County Derry:

> Between him and us
> A great gulf was fixed where pronunciation
> Reigned tyrannically.[27]

We're also made to feel a long way from the centre in the way the war – which came to Liverpool and flattened much of the city and its docks – is brought home. There are actually explosions in *Distant Voices, Still Lives*. The scene where, as children, Eileen, Tony and Maisie get lost in the chaos and stampede for the shelters is powerful because it's very much at odds with the official version: both in the way she is slapped hard in front of everybody by her father when they are reunited – why did some parents used to belt their children out of sheer relief upon finding them after a scare? – and the way in which the sheltering half-heartedly take up the

Eileen, Tony and Maisie as children during Liverpool's Blitz

tremulous 'Roll Out the Barrel' she has been ordered to sing as the bombs thud above them. This is all a long way from the 'spirit of the Blitz', and, indeed, many British cities that were bombed heavily are said to have harboured a resentment at how their travails were overshadowed by what was happening in the skies over London.

The triangulation of banter between Eileen and her friends Micky (played by Debi Jones) and Jingles (Marie Jelliman) is one of the absolute delights of the film. It's all there: the cadences, the rhythms, the mad demotic and dialect words and catchphrases from popular song or the movies. It all sounds so much more *real* than earnest voice-coaching; the depiction of this banter actually revealing the sophisticated layers that make up ordinary everyday speech, where idiolects and shibboleths and song and film dialogue are all woven together and held in play. They also swear like troopers.

As an accent and dialect, Liverpool English, or *scouse*, is still thriving. Scouse – meaning all things Liverpool – only really came into use after the war. So when Tony is locked in the guardhouse with his 'gob iron', it is entirely accurate that he should be asked to 'Play Limelight, Scouse'. The word has a nautical dimension: it is thought to be a contraction of 'lob-scouse', a pot dish made with meat and ship's biscuit. I've often wondered what scouse would be like made with this: I imagine a rock hard, bone-shaped dog biscuit might work, but I've never tried it. I doubt that scouse is actually cooked much any more, even in Liverpool. Unlike, say, bouillabaisse (from Marseille), the dish hasn't entered the culinary canon. Once people in this very small region stop making it, it will become extinct, or uncooked.

When I tell my friends I'm cooking scouse for them, they sometimes ask me if it will be made with stolen ingredients; if I'll be bringing it to table in hub-caps; even if 'cooking scouse' is a euphemism for the preparation of crack cocaine. I take a dim view of such hilarity, and tell them scouse has much older, deeper resonances than that. While the accent and idiom the dish has given its name to might have been mediated to a noisy racket over time, the dish itself has etymological links with the 'labskaus' still eaten in Denmark and Germany, the 'lobskaus' known to Norwegians, and chimes with the Welsh 'lollylobs'. All are one-pot, meat-based stews (though scouse can be served 'blind'). All are thrifty, in that the raw ingredients are basically root vegetables, cheap cuts of meat, perhaps some barley and stock. Scouse, like the accent it has given its name to, is an amalgam of Lancashire (hotpot) and Ireland (stew), with lots of other ingredients thrown in. There is no edible scouse in *Distant Voices, Still Lives*, though pea wack does get a look in.

Depending on where you are, accent confers insiderdom or it excludes you from the club. We should also bear in mind that Davies himself developed an accent altogether different from his peer group, which marked him out; he was bullied mercilessly at school for four years. But the accent had to be right. Davies has proved himself a stickler for details. When he was shooting his version of Edith Wharton's *The House of Mirth* in Scotland, he was troubled by the birdsong picked up in the outdoor scenes; so troubled, in fact, that he overdubbed the Caledonian ornithology with their North American counterparts:

I fear I'm a pedant … [Laughter] … but I do like it to be accurate. I just do. It's like rhythm. People who're not from Liverpool don't get the rhythm, and I say: 'Don't try and do the accent. If you can't get the accent, flatten the vowels, and no-one will know.' Freda [Dowie, who plays the mother] can't do a Liverpool accent, she can't, but if you flatten the vowels … and as long as you get the rhythm right, no one will notice … I was brought up to do things properly. It didn't matter whether you got paid or got extra money. You did them properly. And I remember when I was working for an accountancy firm, and when you do an audit you have lots and lots of working papers, and then you do an analysis of the books, which I then re-wrote. And my boss, who was a lovely man called Mr Taffs, said: 'There's no need to do all this … .' And I said: 'No Mr Taffs. They've got to be done properly. And if someone comes next year to do the audit, they can see what I've done.' I can't just do it slapdash. I can't. Because I think craft is important, and craft means taking the time about doing things properly. And I know it gets on other people's nerves, because they think it's me being finicky. But if it's wrong, it's wrong. And I know that it's wrong.

Just before Tony's wedding in *Still Lives*, his brother-in-law George asks him, 'Well – aul' arse – you ready?'. This is a common enough phrase in Liverpool, but not one that has travelled. Along with 'up the dancers', meaning stairs. Unlike some of the demotic words and phrases that have done well enough on the export market, and found themselves mediated to a much larger Anglophone world, a few have resisted for whatever reason, and hearing these being broadcast in any medium is always a private thrill, as well as a stamp of absolute authenticity. The only other time I've smiled with recognition in the cinema at so many of these signifiers was while watching a very different picture set in Liverpool: Frank Clarke's *Blonde Fist* (1991). At one point, that film's warring heroine (played by the incomparable Margie Clarke) asks one of her offspring to go home and 'put those spuds on a low light'. Perfect. Because *Distant Voices, Still Lives* feels big enough to admit the awkward, uncomfortable words and phrases, too, and not just a kind of self-parodying, simulacrum of voice and speech, it has both alacrity and bite. More importantly, it resists a general move in language towards the clear and distinct that erodes the history contained in words and voices, and renders their former speakers silent.

By the time *Distant Voices, Still Lives* was being made in the mid-1980s, the sound of Liverpudlian voices was no big deal in British culture. Following the Merseybeat explosion of the early 1960s, the trend for all things Liverpool, the Mersey poets and twenty-odd years of television series and soap operas and plays set in Liverpool, the country – indeed, the world – had got used to hearing the accent and some of its particular idioms. I had convinced myself that the accent has changed, within my lifetime: that a kind of media signal of itself has fed back onto the tongue, creating a kind of harsh fizz and disturbance. But linguists are sure that the accent, while it *is* changing, is proving remarkably durable and resistant to influences from other accents, the glottal stop and the dread Esturial creep. That the voices in *Distant Voices, Still Lives* sound in some way to issue from a 'golden age' of Liverpudlian speech is probably just a trick of memory,[28] though I'm sure it was – to use Paul Du Noyer's phrase – more of a 'warm, thick and loamy blend' in the past.

Voices in this film are constantly slipping from their frame. We're alerted to this as viewers very early on, watching an empty staircase while hearing footsteps and voices descending it, and it's a logic we learn to follow. Voices are often heard bleeding out from beyond their frames, and so a new scene will often begin in voiceover before we have left the preceding scene visually. Cinema has frequently employed striking juxtapositions between sound and image, but as a kind of analogue to the opening shipping forecast in *Distant Voices*, followed by these ghostly footfalls, I sometimes think of that scene in *The Cruel Sea*, when the sailors are in the water after abandoning the stricken corvette *Compass Rose* – the classic 'staying awake in the life raft' scene – where the director juxtaposes sound and image very effectively. The drowning and freezing mariners in the cold, black North Atlantic seem to be hearing the voices of their loved ones on land, making tea, sat next to fires or radios. The difference with Davies's film is that, rather than use such slippages to emphasise a key dramatic moment of flashback or reflection, he builds extensive sequences throughout the film out of such tensions between what we see and what we hear.

Frames

'Life stand still here.'

Virginia Woolf, *To the Lighthouse*

Because the camera is so often situated directly in relation to the spaces of the house, its rooms and hall and windows, the film is full of frames-within-frames. So we see the front of the house; the photograph of the father hanging on the parlour wall; the mother sat on the window-ledge cleaning an upstairs window or in the doorway scrubbing the step; the front door and hallway feature in so many scenes. Even while the soundtrack is out of synch with what's happening on screen, creating new ironies or tensions, the picture frame of the film is composed with a huge assurance, favouring these strong orthogonal and rectilinear shapes within it.

When the camera is moving, as in the long tracking shots that have become something of a signature style for Davies, the frame often retains this powerful sense of proportion and composition. Against the big diffused light box of an alehouse window, Eileen is crying and being comforted by Tony. The camera begins to track, slowly, to the left. We pass the glow of another big window, the lit pub doorway and a passageway to the side of the pub with a point of light at the end of it. Then darkness. Next, a stand of lit candles with a plaster Virgin track into view, together with a young Eileen and her family, saying Christmas prayers. The camera keeps moving to the left into darkness again, then fades up tracking past the lit windows of terraced houses, each with its cache of modest decorations. It's a stunning progression, and on the big screen the projected windows have a kind of aquarium glow, snow on the ledges rich against the warmth of each interior we pass. There's a beautiful play between the strict sense of a single pictorial plane and a sense of depth and texture within it.

A track is incredibly powerful and intimate. It draws you into the film emotionally: the relationships change between the space and you … Because we read from left to right, a camera track left to right indicates a forward movement; a track in the opposite direction suggests a journey back in time.[29]

Music also plays a huge role. In the scene just described, the beginning of the long track from right to left feels even more like falling into the past, because the movement is accompanied by the Christmas carol 'In the Bleak Mid-Winter', which seems to turn an emotional motor; the visual passage from dark back into light and image is coterminous with lulls and swells in the choir of voices we hear. This extended passage back into childhood Christmases ends with a frozen scene at the dinner table that erupts all the more savagely in the vacuum after the carol has ended.

Distant Voices, Still Lives is also full of sets: twos, threes, fours. People – often the women – find themselves facing camera grouped in pairs or trios. Aside from the better-known images of the family lined up for wedding and funeral, we see Eileen and Micky paired on the front doorstep, both dressed in Monica Howe's gorgeous white evening dresses, having one last ciggie; we see Eileen, Micky and Jingles craning into the camera-as-mirror, applying their lipstick ('Kiss me you fool'); we see the same trio decked out in blacks and whites, ready to face the onslaught of waiting on tables in Phwelli (for me, this image, along with others in the film, bears an interesting resemblance to the photography of Bill Brandt: in this case, his 'Parlourmaids Ready to Serve Dinner' from 1933); sisters Eileen and Maisie cry together in the dark of the cinema, which cuts to a screen divided into two panels, into which two men fall. Was Davies aware he was doing this?

Not consciously. But in a large family, people do pair off, they just do, it's one of those things. You would always see your sisters' friends, it was always twos or fours, or it could have been three, that's just what it was like. Because I was the youngest, I was sort of outside as well. When the nearest one to you is four years older, seven to eleven seems really grown up, particularly my brothers, because they were all big, and I was the weedy one. So that's completely unconscious, as unconscious as the lists. It's just what I remember. What's always interesting is what you remember subconsciously, because you don't know its function, you just remember it.

One of the most commented upon effects – of lining people up in the same plane facing the camera – is the way that some shots resemble still photographs, especially in the early group scenes in *Distant Voices*. Some of these assemblages have been likened to pictures in an album (though, of course, this way of viewing only really makes sense with the wedding groups: one later scene does actually show the wedding party holding still – 'Smile!' – for a shot that startles the posed with its flash and bulb pop). Slowing the image down to a stasis like this does something to our sense of time in the film. Instead of offering a representation of movement, as memories replayed or 'come to life', stilled images invoke the photograph, and seem to *contain* time.

Davies has spoken of his sense of the 1950s as slow. Of Sunday lunchtimes when 'you could open the window and feel that the whole world was listening to the Light Programme'.[30] If anything, the scene where the funeral party is assembled facing the camera isn't a 'slowing down' – we see the group at a standstill to begin with – but a sudden animation as they rise and leave the frame. This play between stillness and movement in cinema was an important early draw for audiences, keen to see the stilled world they were becoming accustomed to viewing photographically brought to life: very early screenings, a long time before opening credits, simply projected a frozen frame onto the screen, which would then miraculously 'come to life' as the projector was cranked. Our fascination with stasis and motion is still alive and well – or at least has been given a new lease of life, thanks to computerised effects like the whiplash pan – and to be found in films such as *The Matrix* (1999).[31]

It's become virtually impossible not to mention the ideas of either Roland Barthes or Susan Sontag when we enter into this territory: both of their works on photography have proved incredibly convincing and durable.[32] Barthes in particular noticed the difference between the still and moving image as something that 'has posed' before the camera and something that 'has passed' before the camera. A film, like any work of art or literature or music, has to have a life of its own to lead, but Davies is sceptical about any deliberate aim to produce an aesthetic of the photo album on his part, for a number of reasons:

Because we didn't have a camera. We couldn't afford one. There was one Box Brownie in the street. We didn't own it. No, that's the way I saw it. I never thought of it as a sort of *tableau vivant*. That's just how I saw it. When there were big rituals, like weddings or funerals, and you were waiting for the cars, people *did* stand around, I mean, not in a line – fair enough – but they did stand and wait. So that was my remembrance of it, and obviously it's become refracted because of that. People don't actually stand like that, in the parlour … but in your memory they might have done.

The newel-post: a strange beacon of endurance

To say the director here 'aims at influencing the aesthetics of reception by rendering impossible a conventionally narrative decoding of the movie'[33] is to acknowledge some unconscious intention, perhaps, but neglects Davies's aesthetic intentions and the constructed-ness of his film. Things become even more complicated, though, when we consider the photograph of Davies's father on the parlour wall. Here we have a family group, posing very still, and within this 'static' colour shot a still black-and-white photograph (it is the only photograph of Davies's father that exists: he was a rag-and-bone man, and we see him in the street holding onto a horse). The camera slowly zooms in towards this real photograph, and the family walk out of shot away from it. This has precipitated much speculation on the use of 'real' photography within cinematography, even locating a *punctum* within this image.[34]

But if you're going to honour this well-known idea from Barthes's *Camera Lucida*, the notion of *punctum* has to have an element of personal fascination, outside of a cultural or learned response, and if *Distant Voices, Still Lives* has a *punctum* – and I think films, like poems, can have *punctums* – for me it's the newel-post at the foot of the stairs that we see in so many scenes. Phallic, to state the blindingly obvious, but strangely invisible until considered – perhaps because difficult to name – it is there in the opening hallway scene (I can't be the only person who sees its lighthouse shape, with the shipping areas being intoned in the background), there as the father attacks the mother in the hallway (a symbol of rectitude), and there in a shot of the empty hallway after Tony has left for church on his wedding day (veiled with coats hung over it – and this is edited into the veiled bride walking down the aisle!). I see it as the still centre of the film: a strange beacon of endurance.

What interests me about Davies's visual style is his sense of what's happening in the frame as pictorial, whether the camera is moving or not. In respect of his approach to film-making, it's as if photographic and painterly qualities, movement and stillness, are all part of one continuum of images. It's a small point, but I think a fundamental one: Davies simply doesn't respect the boundaries between still photography and cinematography and painting. Of course, it goes without saying that he knows they exist discretely as qualitative things, but putting a frame around the world for the first time was unusually liberating:

I looked down the camera for the first time, and I don't even remember what shot it was, and I thought: 'This is what I was meant for. Even if I do it badly, this is it.' It was the first time I'd looked down ... Because I'd never *made* anything, I'd never even taken stills photographs. It was a revelation.

This sudden insight into a way of framing and building a world from light and texture gives Davies's films a bracingly untrammelled attitude to influence, and what might prove useful in his work. For example, Vermeer (repeatedly cited by Davies as an inspiration and exemplar) is important for a number of reasons. There is, of course, the staging of interior spaces, and often the location of a female presence within such a space. (Though there are exteriors of the house too, especially at the opening and close of *Distant Voices*, where it stands framed on the same plane as *A Street in Delft* [1657–8].) And there are many other formal similarities visible across the centuries and mediums: look at the texture found in the aprons

A Young Woman Standing at a Virginal, Johannes Vermeer, c. 1670–2, oil on canvas (National Gallery, London)

The mother, caught in frames

of carpet or wall hangings found in the darker areas of Vermeer; and look, too, at the painter's predilection for 'frames within frames', for hanging a painting or mirror or map within the picture plane, most obviously echoed in this film by the use of the photograph of the father on the wall.

The shot of the mother on her knees cleaning in the doorway – like the image of her cleaning the upstairs windows, backlit by the sun's radiance – does seem to echo her straitened circumstances by using the frame within the frame. Again, it also brings to mind a Bill Brandt photograph from 1937 of a young housewife in Bethnal Green – indeed, it could be its reverse shot. Tony is moved almost to tears as he asks her when she'll be breaking to have her tea.

And there is another point of intersection, between still photographs and painting, which we could consider. Speaking of early photography, Emile Orlik said:

The expressive coherence due to the length of time the subject had to remain still is the main reason why these photographs ... resemble well drawn or painted pictures and produce a more vivid and lasting impression on the beholder than more recent photographs.[35]

Even when considering cinematography, I don't think it entirely inconceivable that the tiniest movements in frame – of posed faces and bodies held still, of the film moving through the gate – create their own texture and painterly effects. Robert Bresson, in *Notes on the Cinematographer*, said: 'Your camera catches not only physical movements that are inapprehensible by pencil, brush or pen, but also certain states of soul recognizable by indices which it alone can reveal.'[36] Stillness twenty-four frames-per-second isn't a still. (The effect has reached some kind of extreme in artist Gillian Wearing's 1996 piece *Sixty Minutes' Silence*, featuring a line-up of police officers holding still agonisingly for an hour.)

This key regard for the effects of light and texture (in all of his work) means Davies is fastidious in his preparation. Before shooting *Distant Voices, Still Lives*, he 'did masses and masses of tests, and tried different stocks as well'. He was interested in the 'look' of the film: not just as something accurately period (though this matters a great deal too) but as something that elicits an emotional response in the viewer; that will make them feel a certain way. The footage of *Distant Voices, Still Lives*, shot using coral filtration, was subjected to a bleach bypass process:

It was invented by Metrocolour. What they do normally is, when they print a film, they take out the silver oxide, but with this process they leave it in, and so it alters the colour. It was first used by Mike Radford in *Nineteen Eighty-Four,* where the bias was blues and greys and reds, but you can use the entire spectrum. Ours was in the brown sector, not sepia, but brown, so you can go from really pink to very, very dark brown. And what it does is it gives it enormous texture. But just using it like that makes the colour very cold, so we had to warm it up, by various processes, one of which was – it was a wonderful idea, I hadn't thought of it because I'm not an art director – but the wallpaper for instance, with those little roses, which was almost exactly the paper we had, you just wash it with yellow and it *pings* up. But it's very warm, and so all the colours, because they're within that range, they all have the warmth of autumnal colours. I like autumnal colours. I don't like bright

colours. So you've got inbuilt warmth anyway, but also it does look period.
Because I didn't want to make it in black and white, because that wouldn't
have been right, but I wanted the colour to have … I feel that as soon as you
see it, emotionally, you know it's time past. It's not conscious.

In the same way as 'sepia' is sometimes used as a lazy shorthand for
'nostalgia' (itself a desperately misunderstood and co-opted term),
'texture' has to mean more than some kind of attention to surface details
in film. Davies's idea of colour producing a response outside the limits of
language is especially germane when we consider the childhood world:
before language has formed our negotiation with it, the world is saturated
in colour. In his next film, *The Long Day Closes*, the absolute fascination
with light striking an object – a fascination an artist like Vermeer reminds
us of afresh, returning us to the world with rinsed vision – reached a kind
of peak (or nadir, to some viewers) with what Davies calls his 'famous – or
infamous – carpet shot' of the light strengthening then fading on the floor.
Haven't we all done this, especially as children? Davies has spoken of the
ability to say important things by concentrating on the small, the
absolutely quotidian, what he has called 'the poetry of the ordinary'. The
effect itself chimes with Laurence Binyon's 'Winter Sunrise':

> Suddenly, softly, as if a breath breathed
> On the pale wall, a magical apparition,
> The shadow of the jasmine, branch and blossom!
>
> It was not there, it is there, in a perfect image;
> And all is changed. It is like a memory lost
> Returning without a reason into the mind …
>
> And it seems to me that the beauty of the shadow
> Is more beautiful than the flower; a strange beauty,
> Pencilled and silently deepening to distinctness.
>
> As a memory stealing out of the mind's slumber,
> A memory floating up from a dark water,
> Can be more beautiful than the thing remembered.

Untitled, by the author,
1986 (lost), oil on canvas

Light entering the aperture of a room takes us back to Vermeer again, who it is thought used the camera obscura to produce his paintings, in an age when the microscopist van Leeuwenhoek was turning his lens on the miniature world contained in a drop of water, and Galileo was pointing his telescope to the heavens. Here again is the house as centre of the universe, where the young Davies spent so much time studying. Which has the effect of turning a room into a kind of camera itself (perhaps especially so, in the absence of a family camera; and in a family where photography is a kind of rarity reserved for wedding groups). And this in itself is something any still photographer would find attractive, as Geoff Dyer has noticed:

At some point all but the most intrepid – and even the most intrepid – photographers are tempted to retreat inside and contemplate the world from their window. If this suggests a return to first principles – one of the very first permanent photographs, a foggy heliograph made by Joseph Niépce in 1826, was of a *View from the Window at Gras* – there is also an etymological inevitability about it. The camera reverts to its origins, returns to the room into which light – and dark – enters.[37]

This becomes etymologically even more interesting when we consider that *stanza* is Italian for room, forming a rickety linguistic tripod between cameras, rooms in a house and verse units in a poem that I wish nevertheless to explore further.

Poetry

'This be the verse you grave for me.'

Robert Louis Stevenson[38]

Poetry and film can be related in a number of different ways. We can say a film is 'poetic' in much the same way other made things can have such a quality attributed to them; we can write poems specifically to work with moving images (a famous example might be W. H. Auden's *Night-Mail*, which he wrote for the GPO Film Unit in 1936); we can talk about poetry as a formative influence upon a film-maker; we can structurally compare the grammar and syntax of cinema to that of written poetry; we can even conceive of written verse as having spatial qualities: especially useful in the case of *Distant Voices, Still Lives*. Poems like houses. Poets themselves have long conceived of their texts spatially, a place the reader can *inhabit*. They have even exploited it. In *The Canonization*, John Donne puns:

> We can die by it, if not live by love,
> And if unfit for tomb or hearse
> Our legend be, it will be fit for verse;
> And if no piece of chronicle we prove,
> We'll build in sonnets pretty rooms;
> As well a well-wrought urn becomes
> The greatest ashes, as half-acre tombs,
> And by these hymns, all shall approve
> Us canonized for love;

This is somewhat different from conceiving of the Euclidean shape poems make *on the page* (though this can often be a frame-within-a-frame). For Wordsworth, this kind of idea could support an entire sonnet argument:

> Nuns fret not at their convent's narrow room;
> And hermits are contented with their cells;
> And students with their pensive citadels;

Maids at the wheel, the weaver at his loom,
Sit blithe and happy; bees that soar for bloom,
High as the highest Peak of Furness-fells,
Will murmur by the hour in foxglove bells;
In truth the prison, unto which we doom
Ourselves, no prison is: and hence for me,
In sundry moods, 'twas pastime to be bound
Within the Sonnet's scanty plot of ground;
Pleased if some Souls (for such there needs must be)
Who have felt the weight of too much liberty,
Should find brief solace there as I have found.

Distant Voices, Still Lives can be described as 'poetic', or of possessing a 'visual poetry' – creating a kind of echo chamber of chimes and oppositions and contrasts is all part of the film's fabric: so, as well as the black car arriving and departing, we see images of candles and electric light; an opening shipping forecast and a closing valedictory darkness. But there are also interesting parallels between the film and textual, lyric poetry. First though, we must acknowledge the importance of poetry as a formative influence, particularly T. S. Eliot's *Four Quartets* (1943), which Davies has revisited since his mid-teens. This poem can be viewed as providing a kind of underlying, organising principle to so much of his work, especially the earlier films in his autobiographical cycle, a continuing exemplar of how time and memory are essentially fluid. On first encountering it, Davies was undoubtedly arrested by the poem, though that meeting was unorthodox:

I knew what the story was [for *Distant Voices, Still Lives*], and I knew it wasn't linear. I knew I wanted it to be about memory; and the great influence for that was Eliot and the *Four Quartets*. When we got our first television, which was in the sixties – in fact I think it *was* 1960 because of the Rome Olympics – over four nights Alec Guinness read it from memory, and I was knocked out. I didn't understand them. You *know*, something, even though you can't explain it, like seeing Chekhov for the first time, *The Seagull* at the Playhouse. And I didn't understand it but I *knew* what it meant and I thought that's it, it's got to be cyclical, it mustn't be linear, it's not a linear story, because I'd heard these stories by memory, but told out of order. Because of course you remember the most vivid ones first and then the less vivid ones.

Ironies abound. Eliot found his way straight into the Davies's living room just at the point in time where *Distant Voices, Still Lives* leaves off (it's difficult to imagine four nights of the *Four Quartets* on any of the many digital channels now; and this was in the era of BBC/ITV two-channel television), broadcast via the medium that was supplanting cinema. It seems significant in some way, too, that the reader was Alec Guinness, who features in some of Davies's most admired films, including *The Ladykillers* (1955) and *Great Expectations* (1946).

   'Time present and time past/Are both perhaps present in time future,/And time future contained in time past': so go the famous lines from 'Burnt Norton', and it's easy to see how enabling this must have been for a film-maker looking to 'begin' memory, to construct memories in time using elision, and to create an effective filmic time. But Eliot's poem doesn't only offer an approach to architecture – it also seems to instruct in the levels of ambiguity that can be suggested and created, and we can see this in *Distant Voices, Still Lives*. When I asked Davies if he had a sense of poetry and cinema as fellow travellers, if there were any comparisons he felt could be fruitfully made, he focused on one particular aspect of their relationship:

In terms of cinematic ambiguity, yes. What could be more ambiguous but more cinematic than: 'The roses had the look of flowers that are looked at'? I mean that's incredibly cinematic. The opening of *Prufrock* is pure cinema. But I would be drawn more to poetry's ambiguity than any kind of structural, visual structural, device. Because I think that's where it's at its most powerful. Again, reading something – you may not know what it means, but you know. I remember the first time I heard *Prufrock* read, again, I didn't understand it, but you know … something extraordinary and exotic and something very strange is being said to you: 'In the room the women come and go/Talking of Michelangelo.' I couldn't tell you what it means, but I *know*. And I love that level of ambiguity …

It struck me as interesting that Davies chose the rose here, a stock symbol in English poetry for centuries. The rose makes some startling appearances in the cinema of mid-century (that Davies would have seen and been well aware of): I'm thinking of the rose in Powell and Pressburger's *A Matter of Life and Death*, which turns miraculously from the black and white of heaven into a worldly Technicolor that the angels are so starved of; or in Gene Kelly's hands during the ballet sequence in *An American in Paris*. I'm also thinking of Bruce Baillie's *All My Life* (1966), a three-minute track of a worn picket fence punctuated by brilliant roses.

But more than this, *Distant Voices, Still Lives* is full of roses: the wallpaper in the rooms of the house is patterned with 'those little roses, which was almost exactly the paper we had', though the texture is carefully burnished, golden, autumnal. 'Flowers that are looked at' are there, on screen, texturing so many of the interior scenes of the film. We should also bear in mind – and I'm not ascribing some conscious overarching design to the director here: so much of any art happens at the instinctive, subconscious level – that the woman who we see Tony courting and then marrying, who is driven away with him at the end in a black marriage car (itself a kind of cinematic parallelism with the hearse that pulls up at the start of the film, as it moves slowly away from us); this woman, who has a modest role but is only ever seen as sunny and optimistic, and who to my eyes offers a kind of redemption, or at least a way out, for Tony; this woman's name is Rose. (And Davies's next film, *The Long Day Closes*, will start with a credit sequence featuring a bunch of red roses in a vase.)[39]

Eliot's poem, of course, is concerned with the qualities and nature of time, but all lyric poetry has an implicit relationship to it. The lyric can be a 'momentary stay against confusion'[40] but also play fast and loose with time. Time in a lyric is the most highly relative of concepts, and poetry is well equipped to drop the reader into the past through the trapdoor of a stanza break; to move steadily through long corridors of blank verse; to step outside its own flow of events. Davies is fascinated by the nature of film time, and the effects achievable by editing:

What does it mean if you dissolve to a flashback, you cut within the flashback, and then you dissolve back again: where has real time gone? Is it in the flashback, or was it before it happened? I love that … It's a wonderful ambiguity, which I don't think anyone has really solved. Or is it parallel time? What time actually is it? And I do find that level of ambiguity incredibly fascinating.

A great deal of poetry, contemporary and otherwise, has this cinematic facility with time and image. The structural analogies between lyric poetry and film are striking, and especially pronounced in the work of a director like Davies, who has a great curiosity regarding time and space. Poetry can even be said to have contained cinematic effects long before the advent of cinema itself. Eisenstein famously wrote of similar effects in the novels of Charles Dickens,[41] and Flaubert's *Madame Bovary* (1857) seems to contain textual examples of voiceover and montage way in advance of the Lumière Brothers. It is easy to find scores of poems that cut to flashbacks, use close-ups next to wide shots and generally deploy – knowingly or instinctively – the syntax and grammar of the cinema. From Jorge Luis Borges haunting the movie houses of 1920s Buenos Airies, to Louis MacNiece escaping the humdrum of a Birmingham lecturing life in the 1930s, the subject is potentially vast, and the conditions of influence subtle and various. In terms of contemporary work, this is hardly surprising, given the century of cinema we've just left. Various attempts to map the overarching relationships between poetry and film have been made: the experimental American film-maker Maya Deren conceived of a 'horizontal' and 'vertical' axis present in film, where the former exists to develop plot, character, drama; while the latter accommodates lyrical investigations.[42] Though the subject is well worth investigating further, it's beyond the scope of this short study, except to notice two more points.

Writing a poem can never be held up in strict analogy to film-making: in a way, all of a poet's experience is potential grist to the mill – *everything* becomes research – and the stages of a film's pre-production – scriptwriting, location scouting, colour stock tests – don't have a strict analogue with what the poet is purposefully doing. But once a draft of the work has been assembled, there are several marked similarities, mostly to do with editing. Colin McCabe, the executive producer of *Distant Voices, Still Lives*, wrote of how any micro-adjustments to the script could have huge repercussions for the whole film,[43] and this sense of absolute interconnectedness would strike a chord with many poets' sense of achieving the poem; how any tiny change in direction can affect the balance of the whole text and the direction it will take. Listening to Davies talking about the relationship between shooting and editing gives a similar sense of the holistically viewed work, as well as indicating the necessary formal pain – surely familiar to all poets – of having to cut ruthlessly. The following passage is interesting, too, because it identifies that leap from the page to the screen, when the shot footage takes on a life of its own:

When you're shooting it, you have to be aware of practical things. You don't start to look at where a shot begins to decay until it's juxtaposed with other things, then you can extend things, or take something out, because it's superfluous to what you're saying, or it's holding up the information that you want to give. It's something that happens after the shot footage is put together. Once I get that first assembly, I never, ever look at the script again, because there's no point: you've got the first assembly, and so now it's got to live, on its own. There are things in the script that work because you are reading them. When they're on screen it's different, because you're seeing it and you're feeling it differently. There was a long sequence in *The House of Mirth*, where it was a continuous track for ten minutes, and we had beautiful weather and they hit all their marks, and it was fabulous. And of course it was completely superfluous. It was very hard to say: 'It's got to go.' But when it was dropped, and we just put it back together, we thought, yeah. All that was in that ten-minute track is said by juxtaposing those two things there. And it's actually better. I learned a very hard lesson when I was at film school. I was doing *Madonna and Child*, and it was shot in Birkenhead, where I worked: my last regular job. And there was a scene, one shot, where he goes across this bridge at magic hour, which is now [September, early evening outside, low sun], sun coming through it, all steel, and it was a ravishing shot. And when we put it together the editor said: 'It's got to go.' It was so hard. But it was right to go.

Within the overarching stylistic and formal qualities, there's also the film's use of lists to consider. The opening's shipping forecast is described by Davies as 'a mantra': it was less important to understand what was being said, than to enjoy – or cling to – the way it was being said, and the familiarity of its speaking voice. The shipping forecast has been recognised by poets, too – ships and lists have gone together since Homer – and its areas have actually made a few appearances in post-war poetry (see, for example, Seamus Heaney's 'Glanmore Sonnets' [1977]), though this listing is just the first of several in the film. On the train with his unit, Tony is going through the list of heavyweight-boxing champions:

> TONY: You're wrong – Schmelling never won the title … the heavyweight champions were Jack Sharkey, Primo Carnera, Braddock, Baer – no, I tell a lie … Baer then Braddock, then Joe Louis …

We see Tony later, sat in an armchair checking the pools coupons, that incantatory index to the British cold-weather months; still audible, though it used to seem as if the world would stop on Saturday, just before five o'clock, to listen to the radio. We also see him listening to the racing results. The ritual of going to the bar involves the litany of ordering a round of drinks:

> TONY: Two halves of shandy. A mackies. A Double Diamond. A pale ale and lime. A Black and Tan. Mild over bitter. A rum and pep. A rum and blackcurrant. And a Guinness.

Tony: list-making and singing

Lists are speech acts that try to impose order; they can also be mantras, spell-like. In *Distant Voices, Still Lives* they are both. These people in this part of the world during these times were not the damned and suffering of the earth – in some ways, their lives were richer than ours – but they lived a fairly precarious existence: dreary manual work for small pay packets at English Electric or Paton Calverts. By the 1950s the sailor in Liverpool was still a kind of small god, but the days of the 'Cunard Yanks' were numbered. Nobody owned property, or amassed savings, or studied share options. Going to university was rare. Nobody had the kind of stable, assured identity reinforced by land ownership or an entry in Debrett's *Peers and Peerage*. This is life being lived from one week to the next: as well as songs and stories, these everyday litanies were part of the fabric that held them together, ensuring them continuity and a sense of themselves.

Music

'Music, companion of joy, medicine for pain.'

Inscription in Vermeer's *Couple Standing at a Virginal*

Pop music as we know it today – a sensual confection of blues and rock and Motown and soul – really got under way in the early 1960s, blowing petrified tradition into a thousand pieces and lighting a fire under chilly post-war austerity. Or at least, that's how the story is most often told. Upon leaving school as a teenager in 1960 (at fifteen, he was told by a man from the Labour Exchange that he was 'office material'), Davies worked just round the corner from Mathew Street in Liverpool. But even though he was so close to ground zero, Davies never visited the 'internationally famous Cavern Club' (his nicely tart author note in *A Modest Pageant* is telling: 1963 as *annus horribilis*). Having imbibed *Ready Steady Go* while *in utero*, I have to confess I love pop. But Davies had already learned to love the Great American Songbook; Nat King Cole, Ella Fitzgerald, the lyrics of Cole Porter, Gershwin, Rodgers and Hammerstein; the Hollywood musicals. He was also just discovering T. S. Eliot, and the classical repertory. First there were school visits to hear the Liverpool Philharmonic Orchestra:

And when I left school I didn't have enough money, because I was only earning two pounds five shillings a week. So I bought my first LP, which was Carl Schuricht conducting the Paris Conservatoire Orchestra, and it was Beethoven's *Fifth Symphony*, and it had a black-and-white photograph of the Parthenon, and it was Ace of Clubs, and it was ten and sixpence. And then I started going. I could afford the industrial concerts … and one drink. Then I started listening to the Third Programme, and then was listening all the time. By the time rock and roll came in, my interest in popular music started to decline. Because, up until then, Cole Porter was still writing. But I remember one of my sisters – I think it was Helen – took me to see *Jailhouse Rock* [Elvis Presley's second film, released in 1957] and I cringed with embarrassment. I thought he had a terrible voice, and I just thought he was ridiculous, and even now I cannot bear to watch him.

Nowadays, every film comes bundled with an original soundtrack release, but music's ubiquity doesn't often equate to integrity of purpose, or simply work to a film's advantage. Employing period music in drama was still arresting in 1988; Dennis Potter's explorations of using music extensively in television drama are worth comparing with Davies's work, especially *The Singing Detective* (1986), but also the less well known *Cream in Your Coffee* he wrote for LWT in 1980, which attempts an elliptical style of its own.

Distant Voices, Still Lives seems to be made of music: it takes up over half of the film's screen time. When I think of the film and try to project scenes from it in my mind (or Priestley's 'skull cinema'), they invariably hang together and make sense as musical sequences: the overture from 'Love is a Many-Splendored Thing'; Ella Fitzgerald's 'Taking a Chance on Love'; Vaughan Williams's Pastoral Symphony No. 3, luminous and yearning as the camera rises slowly in front of the dark terraced house at night; any of the smoky relays of pub sing-alongs; Peter Pears singing 'O Waly, Waly' as the newlyweds, then the family itself, disappear into the dark:

I think film is closest to music, of all the art forms. The reason I think it's closest to music is because when you listen to music you respond viscerally. I can only speak as a non-musician, I don't play anything, and I sing in the key of zed … [laughter] … but you believe or you don't believe. You don't even have to think about it, you either believe or you don't. *Nothing* will induce me to listen to Wagner. I just think, I'm bored to tears. And it goes on for literally *days*. Life's too short. But once you believe, you can follow the musical argument, even if you're not a musician. You feel. That's what you do. You feel instinctively with music.

In the same way that colour and texture create mood and emotion, music triggers its own visceral responses in the viewer; but it also does so much more. Ella Fitzgerald's 'Taking a Chance on Love' plays to a scene of appalling violence: the song's optimism and romanticism (and sense of going round in circles and of having been here before: 'Here I slide again/About to take that ride again,/Starry eyed again/Taking a chance on love') put through the wringer in a powerful juxtaposition. The popular music that saturates the film as much as any coral filter means viewers are not only offered an accurate period 'sound world' to inhabit, but are also invited to bring their own memories to the table: music, of course, being a swift and devastating vector of buried thoughts, able to tap down and excavate forgotten corners with the efficacy of an old perfume. This is sometimes mistaken for nostalgia, but the tension created in the scene just described – and there are many more instances in this director's work – means the past contains unfinished business:

One reason is that this material is not dead but overpoweringly alive. For Davies the past is not a foreign country in the sighing, elegiac sense coined in *The Go-Between* … For Davies, if the past is a foreign country, it's guerrilla territory: not a sedate outpost of our existential empire but a Vietnam of the mind.[44]

If *Distant Voices, Still Lives* were further distilled and stripped down, I'm convinced we'd end up with a film like Bruce Baillie's difficult-to-see *All My Life*, which consists, in its entirety, of a track from right to left along a worn Californian picket fence to the sound of Ella Fitzgerald singing 'All My Life', accompanied by Teddy Wilson and His Orchestra. This work can be viewed as an extremely minimalist version of Davies's film: the essential

The author's mother (left) and friend, Liverpool, early 1960s.

track into the past (in this case, from 1960s 'happening' America back into the Depression Era), with a strict pop musical imperative, the sense of colour and texture, even roses.

Popular music is most strongly associated with Eileen and Micky and Jingles in the film: their very speech is liable at any moment to burst into lyrics, actual or corrupted; they are willing visitors to this parallel universe of rainy 1950s Merseyside. We're asked to understand this, because this is how it was, and perhaps still is to some extent. The music is never called in as reinforcement for the narrative, or used as a simplistic ornamental veneer. The pub was the communal space where singing broke out and was general:

It's a generational thing. I think it probably started to change mid- to late 60s. But the people who went to pubs and sang like that, they were a generation who knew lyrics as something that were meant to be sung by other people, not just the people who recorded them. They were proper songs. Can you really have a sing-along to 'Hey Jude'? They could still be called traditional lyrics, but that wasn't popular music's function any more. Its function was something to move around to, not to actually listen to the lyric and sing it yourself. That changed. And now you can't hear the lyric at all.

The atmosphere in a room: sunny ...

And when you can they're unbelievably stupid. Who could write a witty song? Nobody. There's no equivalent of Cole Porter. There's no equivalent of Rodgers and Hammerstein ...

As we've seen, it is music that so often determines the very rhythm and shape of the film. When the family and friends are in the pub singing 'I Love the Ladies', see how the film cuts from one couple to another, and how within each of these shots the singers address the group or each other:

I can remember Bill Diver saying, 'I want to cut against the rhythms,' and I said, Fine, but I reserve the right to say no. And he cut against the rhythm and found it was a mess! Because my underlying rhythm is not fast. There was another moment when he was cutting, when they were singing 'I Love the Ladies'. That cut is the first cut: he caught it fabulously, but the underlying tempo is actually slow, it's not fast. It appears to be, but it's not. But he caught the underlying rhythm while still doing a lot of cuts within that short bit of song. But it was fabulous. I said 'Don't touch it.' Perfect. It gets all the right elements in the right order.

This is the alehouse before jukeboxes and games machines ate into its spaces. People find this unbearably nostalgic. Nobody really sang in the pub like this, did they? By the time I was taken into pubs, the knees-up had mostly ended, though you would get the odd flare-up at closing time. The bingo became hugely popular in the 1960s and 1970s (my mother went each week with the sister of Michael Starke, who plays Dave in the film), and the distaff side stopped singing . But they really did once. I suppose it depends upon how willing you are to believe that drink and song and the moment can feel like enough: can feel like home. I don't think this is a straightforward rehearsal of some lost community: the immersion into song – the sense of belonging in the moment that only works if everyone joins in – is broken sometimes ('I've got good reason to, you shithouse!'); or it acts like a chorus of voices taking an idea into another dimension: watch how Doreen, who has come to mind Maisie's baby, crosses the threshold and enters the house just as Eileen, singing 'Brown Skinned Girl', starts up ('Brown skinned girl stay home and mind baby'). The cast had to be taught most of the lyrics:

I got my family to sing them, on tapes. It was difficult, actually, knowing what to leave out. Because if I'd put everything in, people wouldn't have believed it, so I had to pare down what had happened. All the songs that I'd heard them sing, that were my favourites, I put in. It was as simple as that. None of them knew any of the lyrics. Their parents did …

There is a great moment in *Still Lives* – just after a fracas has been narrowly averted between an aggrieved Dave ('No one knows what's goin' on in my head!') and Eileen ('Includin' you!'), who is sticking up for the recently thwarted Jingles – when Micky breaks into song after Mrs D. has intervened. Red gives her a look; he seems to breathe a sigh of relief with his eyes, thankful for Micky's way of being in the world, and for his union with her. Which he then proceeds to suppress with a ribbing ('Oh, eh Mick … Yer not singin' again?'): overenthusiastic shows of feeling are held in check, though aggression sometimes breaks the surface; nobody cracks out of turn; singing is the vehicle for communal expression.

… but suddenly changeable and overcast

There is also symphonic sense to consider. The film as a whole has a refreshing catholicity, and music and speech from different cultural idioms happily co-habit. Davies has often spoke of his appreciation of classical music – especially Bruckner and Sibelius – and his belief that movement in film has a great deal to learn from symphonic movement:

And that's why I think if you can follow a symphonic argument, and you're not a musician, then you should be able to go on that same symphonic journey, but with film. One thing that complicates it is, you have talk: that does complicate the issue. Because you can mislead with dialogue, when you don't intend to. When you do mean to, that's wonderful, but sometimes that can be a real pitfall. You can see a wonderful cinematic idea ruined by bad dialogue. But I still come back to what I said originally: I do believe music and cinema are absolutely close, and when you have the right image with the right music, there's *nothing* more thrilling. I remember when we were doing the overhead shots for the end of *The Long Day Closes*, and it was already written for 'Tammy', and we did the first overhead shot, and as soon as you heard that playback the whole crew lifted like this … It was *magical*. And then when I saw it put together I knew it would work, I knew in my heart.

The underlying tempi of Davies's films are slow: in this respect they feel completely at odds with so much contemporary work, pumped with the accelerants of audience expectation and an absolute fear of the meditative: 'I don't like spurious cutting. It's like modern television drama, they think lots of things happening is drama, it's not. It's just lots of things happening.' Composers such as Bruckner are capable of taking the listener on a real journey, *if* the listener has the patience and ability to invest in the work. Deeply unfashionable. But this slowness invites the viewer really to look, to inhabit. Writing on Vermeer's *Couple Standing at a Virginal*, Pierre Descargues observed how the painting's space could be inhabited so convincingly that 'simply by sitting down on the floor we should find ourselves at the heart of the picture': compare this with Bresson's call for a cinema of total immersion: 'Your film is not made for a stroll with the eyes, but for going right into, for being totally absorbed in.'[45]

So Davies's film has huge underlying musical imperatives – he seems to conflate cinema and music to a degree few other directors have attempted or managed – but his approach to sound in general is innovative. His radio montages work brilliantly: so Uncle Ted descends the stairs to ' … your speaker, The Man in Black … ' or George dozes as *The Billy Cotton Band Show* strikes up its 'Wakey! Way-kee!'. ('Hey you! You down there with the glasses!' is accompanied by a radiophonic tunnelling sound that rises in pitch: it sounds like a satellite going up into space, the sound of history getting into the living room.) Building this kind of a fabric from sound looks towards the opening sequence of his next film, *The Long Day Closes*. We tend to regard the 1940s and 1950s, from our early twenty-first-century vantage point, as austere and static, especially compared to our culture in perpetual motion, with its sound and image saturation and ever-shifting mediums and formats. But this would be wrong, I think. The radio and cinema were ubiquitous, and while there may not have been the sheer amount of material on offer, exposure to such sources was woven into the fabric of everyday life. The 1950s was a time of great change in cinematographic terms; recorded music was in the process of shifting from mono to stereophonic releases; television was beginning its long process of supplanting radio (and cinema, for that matter) as the dominant mass medium. So anybody in Britain living through the 1950s would have had their sense of the world constantly and subtly enlarged and mediated. The movies themselves took on television – and lost. They had yet to work out how to synergise and collude with the newer medium.

Movies

'You're nothing but a shadow on film ... You're not flesh and blood.'
Debbie Reynolds in *Singin' in the Rain* (1952)

In the same way that the young Herman Melville claimed a whaling ship was his Yale and Harvard, Terence Davies received much of his schooling in the constellation of cinemas that thrived for a while in post-war Liverpool. This director is equipped with a capacious knowledge of movies, and watched anything and everything indiscriminately and voraciously. This aspect of Davies's childhood and youth is more thoroughly explored in the film he made after *Distant Voices, Still Lives*: *The Long Day Closes*. That film sees a return to a central persona based, to some degree, upon aspects of Davies's biography that he had also used in each part of his *Trilogy*.

Bud is obsessed with 'the pictures'. But any of Davies's films – and *Distant Voices, Still Lives* is certainly no exception – betrays this knowledge of cinema, and, perhaps more importantly, a passion for the medium:

Kensington, Liverpool, c. 1950s (Courtesy of Liverpool Record Office)

Someone years later sent me a picture of Kensington Street and it looked so dreary, I cannot tell you how uninteresting it seemed, but it didn't to me when I was growing up. I had an intense relationship with the house and the street and the environment. It all felt part of the same thing; the intimacy of the home, then your street, then the streets around, the streets you took to go to school, and then the streets that you took to go to church, and the streets that you took to the eight cinemas that were around me. I always went the same way to every cinema, and I could traverse those same streets now. I can still remember where I saw certain films, where I sat, who I went with. It's *still* that vivid.

The movies offered escape, either from an oppressive household or just the mundane offices of the working week. We only see one (unforgettable) scene at the cinema in *Distant Voices, Still Lives*, but its influence, along with that of radio, is constantly palpable, in the air, and sets up a tension between, on the one hand, glamour, snappy dialogue and song; and on the other, bad marriages, low-wage households, rain. In this film, the cinema is a space where the women go, and can weep outside the necessary stoicism of their domestic roles. It's almost impossible to imagine Pete Postlethwaite in this context. When Maisie asks her mother: 'Why did you marry him, Mam?', her reply, at that point in the film, throws these discrepancies into strongest relief: 'He was nice, he was a good dancer.'

Davies was visiting the flicks religiously just as Hollywood's studio system was winding down. (A distant contemporary, Rainer Werner Fassbinder, was doing exactly the same thing, haunting the Bavarian picture houses of the 1950s.) André Bazin had already observed how the quality of Hollywood was borne of a sense of tradition:

The American cinema is a classical art, but why not then admire in it what is most admirable, i.e., not only the talent of this or that filmmaker, but the genius of the system, the richness of its ever-vigorous tradition, and its fertility when it comes into contact with new elements.[46]

By the beginning of the 1960s, every city's geography of Futurists and Gaumonts and Essoldos and Odeons was falling on harder times. In

Liverpool, the packed and smoky dream palaces, glimpsed in *Distant Voices, Still Lives* and explored more thoroughly in *The Long Day Closes*, were turning into fleapits – their plush stained with sherry, burned with ciggies – showing B-movies and horror flicks. Some were being pulled down. That strangely bereft opening to the latter film – a street left to ruin, gone to seed, filled with the disembodied sounds of cinema – could be one of the once busy standing lots at MGM or RKO *if* their last picture had been set in a northern English street.[47]

'New York Street' was MGM's busiest standing lot, where Stanley Donen and Gene Kelly shot *that* sequence in *Singin' in the Rain* (Davies's favourite film). How much has this, and all of those other films he saw, influenced Davies? Greatly, I'd suggest, but at such an unconscious, instinctive level that it would be remiss to start attributing direct links. Just in terms of colour and 'look', the rich, saturated hues of three-strip Technicolor, the depth and chiaroscuro created in films like *Singin' in the Rain*[48] or Minnelli's *Meet Me in St Louis* (1944), or in MacKendrick's *The Ladykillers*, must have burnt in deep against the grey maritime world outside. But black-and-white films, such as *Kind Hearts and Coronets* (1949) or *The Night of the Hunter* (1955), have also been cited by the director, from time to time, as significant. This sense of 'texture' again is all-important:

It's about what texture does. It makes you respond in a way, however vague that way is. For instance, I was watching *Separate Tables* a couple of days ago; you see the exterior of this hotel, which has been built in the studio – it's wonderfully art-directed, fabulous hotel, I'd have loved to have lived there – you see this in a wide shot, it's in black and white, very soft black-and-white, and the credits roll, and you hear Vic Damone singing. And you are immediately … It's not what you're looking at, or what you hear, it's the way in which that black and white view of that hotel makes you feel. And when you juxtapose it with a romantic song sung by an American, it makes you feel different, because it's clearly not a romantic hotel. It's Eastbourne, and it's all old, and most of the residents are old. But it makes you *feel* in a certain way. And *that's* what texture does.

Beyond being an exemplar of texture, Delbert Mann's 1958 film is also interesting for its sense of a constructed interior space (in this case, the fading Hotel Beauregard); the manager, played by Wendy Hiller (who won an Academy Award for her role), is forever opening and closing windows and doors and screens, sealing off rooms, creating frames within frames, new spaces.

But *Distant Voices, Still Lives* is exciting because it's roomy enough to accommodate Dickie Valentine *and* Vaughan Williams, Billy Cotton *and* Benjamin Britten. We need to appreciate Davies's instinctive refusal to erect barriers between aspects of culture: he is receptive to all of the Hollywood musicals he repeatedly saw *and* Ingmar Bergman, Ealing comedies *and* Orson Welles. Davies has often been regarded as part of an auteur tradition, described as having much in common with European film-makers (and Jean-Luc Godard's claim that, apart from *Distant Voices, Still Lives*, 'the British were never very gifted movie-makers' might constitute assent from the horse's mouth).[49] A couple of examples: Ingmar Bergman's *Cries and Whispers* (1972) appears to be an important film for Davies (I seem to remember him introducing a screening of it on BBC television in the early 1990s), and isn't it possible to discern its influence, especially in *Still Lives*, with all that red livery in the alehouse, and those searing fades into white that take us out of time in much the same way as when Bergman floods his screen with crimson? (In a short interview for *Sight and Sound* in January 2003, Davies explained how that scene where Harriet Andersson seems to reawaken from the dead while laid out powerfully evokes his memory of having to sleep in his recently dead father's bed when he was a child.) Robert Bresson, too – while not picked

up in director polls by *Sight and Sound* or *Time Out*[50] – must register as more than a bat-squeak: look at the very first scene in the pub, where the group are singing 'If You Knew Suzie', and the pan away from the serving hatch that shows us the assembled boozers only as hands and torsos, before meshing into the singers' faces at seated height; although, as someone wryly remarked to me when pointing this out, Bresson probably wouldn't have panned.

Bresson meets Coronation Street?

The demise of studio pictures happened at the same time as the *Cahiers*-inspired French New Wave and British 'kitchen sink' realism were in the ascendant. Life amid northern terraces and factories and pubs was already becoming the subject of movies such as *Saturday Night and Sunday Morning* (Karel Reisz, 1960), *A Taste of Honey* (Tony Richardson, 1961), *A Kind of Loving* (John Schlesinger, 1962) and *This Sporting Life* (Lindsay Anderson, 1963). All this 'realism' and subject matter might have come as a contrast to the kind of cinema that had preceded it, but Davies hasn't acknowledged a great debt to, or affection for, this work generally. Speaking in 1990 he gave one hint as to the reason why:

There's never been any film which has really done it ... So it's seeing little bits of little films that you think, 'Yes, that little scene captured just something, an echo of what it was like.' But I can't think of any film that really captured what it felt like to be working class, because working-class people didn't make movies.[51]

There is also documentary to consider, from the work of John Grierson and Humphrey Jennings in the 1930s to the Free Cinema movement in the mid- to late 1950s. The latter movement – like Davies – looked to Europe and aspects of Hollywood, but was a movement, with a theoretical exoskeleton, a manifesto. Perhaps the greatest influence on Davies was the sense of Hollywood moving away from the sound stage and the back lot to locations: the 'real thing'. Probably the most difficult aspect of moviegoing for us to understand now – especially for the likes of me, born during or after the 1960s – is its sense of continuum with the quotidian. It might be overly simplistic to portray cinema as straightforwardly escapist, though there was undoubtedly an element of this. Many of those stars we now view from our own ironic plateau – tainted or discredited in an age of biography and exposé – were once viewed as emblematic and exemplary and honourable; a view reinforced by family, street, school. 'The Yanks have colonized our subconscious,' says one of the projector technicians in Wim Wenders's *Kings of the Road* (1976); but their movies also reinforced – for better or worse – an order, a fabric of life:

Once you get to the 1960s, and they're starting to shoot in real locations, then the films that will be made will be different. Those hermetically sealed films have, for me ... I've been thinking about this a lot recently ... They have a *glow* that modern films don't have, they never will. And we don't have stars now, we have accountants, and people making a lot of money. But they're not stars. They come on, and you wonder: 'I wonder why he gets twenty million dollars a picture.' But I saw that transition from hermetically sealed, studio-bound pictures, to it starting to become ... more real. And we're now seeing the end of that realism, where subtlety goes out the window. And I'm not saying an awful lot of terrible films weren't made under the studio system: there were. Bloody awful. And I sat through a lot of them. But if I had to choose between a hermetically sealed, sentimental movie, and seeing people being tortured, and people being foul and violent and foul-mouthed, I would choose the former. I had enough of that when I was a kid.

Afterlives

'We see the world once, in childhood.
The rest is memory.'

Louise Gluck[52]

Something fades and passes from the world as we enter into language, and become aware of time, and *Distant Voices, Still Lives*, more than any other film I know, manages to give shape to this most Wordsworthian of tropes; and it does so in an urban context saturated with popular culture. What does it mean to live in such a family, such a class, with our formative years full of music and images? How do we remember, having intimately known the microcosms of our rooms and houses and streets, but *also* the phantoms and chimeras of cinema and radio and television, while we were young and 'living in the moment'? Are such total experiences inauthentic in some way, mere by-products in an age of mechanical reproduction: of no value?

Musical, resonant, multi-layered and inexhaustibly approachable, the film is a space where dissonances meet and harmonise; where influence becomes confluence. It also manages to synthesise memory to an extraordinary degree: looking back is both joyous and painful at once. It is

Newlyweds Rose and Tony being driven away into their future

nostalgia in an etymologically accurate sense – to return home and to suffer pain in some way – though not in a simple-minded, derisive sense: it never hankers after an illusory, idealised past. It deals with a break, an old wound, using stories and memories; it feels as necessary and creaturely as storytelling around a fire. We are remiss not to remember, even though remembering is no aid to 'progress', as Joseph Roth reminds us: 'Everything that existed left behind traces of itself, and people then lived by their memories, just as we nowadays live by our capacity to forget, quickly and comprehensively.'[53]

Perhaps one way of finding out what happened to these people, after they've walked into the darkness at the end of the film, lies in work like Gary Oldman's 1997 film *Nil by Mouth* (which he dedicated to the memory of his father): Kathy Burke's battered, closed-up eyes and obliteration at the hands of a coked-up Ray Winstone does bring to mind Freda Dowie's awful trials; we hear Kern and Hammerstein's 'Can't Help Lovin' Dat Man' sung by a grandmother (just before Cole Porter's 'My Heart Belongs to Daddy', and The Andrews Sisters); there are even pub sing-alongs. Or we could look to photographers: Martin Parr's *Last Resort* (1986) shows Liverpool at play 'over the water' in New Brighton in the mid-1980s: disarray and tackiness verging on squalor; Tom Wood has caught the city looking for love in the 1980s, and from the windows of its buses; or Richard Billingham's *Ray's a Laugh* (1996) and *Black Country* (1997): the former is a series of studies (of the photographer's own family) lit and irradiated by long hours in front of the television, a terminal moraine of white goods and mail order kitsch that was already beginning to mobilise towards the end of the 1950s where Davies's film leaves off. *Black Country* features 'Night Time Two Thousand and Three', a series of nocturnes taken in and around Cradley Heath in the West Midlands, where Billingham grew up: his childhood home. Here are the late-Victorian brick terraces and schools lit by the halogen and sodium of a new century, boarded up or slowly being eaten by British jungle.

At the time of the film's release, in October 1988, I remember reading one of the many reviews, in a broadsheet, that quoted these slightly less famous lines from Philip Larkin's 'This Be the Verse': 'Man hands on misery to man./It deepens like a coastal shelf …'. Larkin's poem *The*

Whitsun Weddings was finished thirty years earlier in October 1958, and I like to imagine that Rose and Tony's marriage, at the end of *Distant Voices, Still Lives*, happened while Larkin was writing it in Hull, at the other end of what was yet to be the M62: Britain's *Alpenstrasse* still a blueprint in municipal offices. As the wedding party breaks up and the last players walk into the dark ground of the celluloid, Peter Pears sings 'O Waly, Waly', leaving a maritime lullaby to echo the shipping forecast's aubade eighty minutes earlier:

> A ship there is, and she sails the sea,
> She's loaded deep as deep can be,
> But not so deep as the love I'm in;
> I know not if I sink or swim.

There is a sense of lives having passed before our eyes, and fading now from view: a way of life, and a way of being in the world, leaving the stage. In many ways, Larkin's train, when we read the poem now, carries a similar weighty cargo: the hopes and ambitions of a generation. I hope – every time I enter the film's time, and it is all yet to happen again – that they are not, somewhere, becoming rain.

Notes

1 All quotes from Terence Davies, unless indicated otherwise, are from an interview with the director that took place on 19 September 2005 at Oscar's, Charlotte Street Hotel, London W1. Our conversation, much of which was recorded, lasted over three hours. Earlier, I had watched *Distant Voices, Still Lives* theatrically at the BFI, so found myself in the ridiculously agreeable situation of walking out into daylight and meeting the director of the film I'd just seen.

2 Terence Davies, *A Modest Pageant* (London: Faber and Faber, 1992) contains the scripts for all Davies's films up to and including *The Long Day Closes*. Essential reading, especially for the director's own illuminating Introduction; the script for *Distant Voices* is preceded by the following note (quoting T. S. Eliot):

NB: *Distant Voices* is about memory and the mosaic of memory.

Father is the central pivot around which Mother, Eileen,
Maisie and Tony revolve and all have equal dramatic weight.

Memory does not move in a linear or a chronological way – its
pattern is of a circular nature, placing events (not in their 'natural'
or 'real' order) but recalled for their emotional importance.

Memory *is* its own validity.

Thus any 'story' involving memory is not a narrative in the
conventional sense but of necessity more diffuse, more elliptical.

Therefore conventional narrative expectation will not be satisfied
in any conventional way, and I would ask you to bear this in mind
when you are reading this piece.

I was trying to create 'a pattern of timeless moments'.

3 Jorge Luis Borges, *Selected Poems 1923 –1967* (London: Allen Lane, 1972). This is from a sonnet called 'Rain', translated by Alistair Reid:

Quite suddenly the evening clears at last
As now outside the soft small rain is falling.
Falling or fallen. Rain itself is something
Undoubtedly which happens in the past.

Whoever hears it falling has remembered
A time in which a curious trick of fate
Brought back to him a flower whose name was 'rose'
And the perplexing redness of its red.

This rain which spreads its blind across the pane
Must also brighten in forgotten suburbs
The black grapes on a vine across a shrouded

Patio now no more. The evening's rain
Brings me the voice, the dear voice of my father,
Who comes back now, who never has been dead.

4 *In Memoriam* was first published anonymously in 1850: 'Dark House' is one of its best-known passages.
5 Davies, *A Modest Pageant*, pp.124–5.
6 Ibid., Introduction, p. xi.
7 See the epigraph to his poem 'True', in *Errata* (Oxford: Oxford University Press, 1993).
8 William Empson, *Collected Poems* (London: Chatto & Windus, 1962).
9 Pedantic friends in the building trade have pointed out that the type of brick, prominent in some threshold shots, is a London stock brick, which itself indicates location.
10 Eva Hoffman, *Lost in Translation* (London: Vintage, 1991).
11 Gaston Bachelard, *The Poetics of Space* (Boston: Beacon Press, 1994). First published in French in 1958 as *La Poétique de l'espace*.
12 W. H. Auden, *About the House* (London: Faber and Faber, 1966).
13 'It is as though we had to describe and explain a building whose upper storey was erected in the nineteenth century, the ground floor dates back to the sixteenth century, and careful examination of the masonry reveals

that it was reconstructed from a tower built in the eleventh century. In the cellar we come upon Roman foundations, and under the cellar a choked-up cave with Neolithic tools in the upper layer and remnants of fauna from the same period in the lower layers. That would be the picture of our psychic structure.' Carl Jung, 'Mind and Earth', in *Civilization in Transition* (Princeton: Princeton University Press, 1970). Though compare this with that scene in Ingmar Bergman's *Fanny and Alexander* (1982), where Alexander is locked in the attic of the bishop's chancery: that space is rendered irrational and creepy in the extreme, as Alexander senses, then sees, dead people (and is itself surely an influence on M. Night Shyamalan's 1999 hit *The Sixth Sense*?).

14 *Letters of Rainer Maria Rilke 1910–1926* (New York: Norton, 1993).

15 Davies has often expressed his admiration of Alexander McKendrick's 1955 film, the last of the Ealing comedies, and it is easy to imagine such a stylised and rich-looking film providing a great influence; *The Long Day Closes* features elements of the soundtrack in its opening montage. Watching it is always an act of time travel for me: when I lived in King's Cross in the early 1990s, my walk to the Underground took me right past the spot where Mrs Wilberforce's house should have stood; every time I see the film now, I'm always surprised by how little the actual area around Argyle Square, looking north to St Pancras station, had changed, with its boarding houses and railings. The view from Mrs Wilberforce's front door looks out onto this area, but her back yard can't really abut the rail lines in and out of King's Cross: this was the site of my flat. If I can be forgiven for making one extremely slender connection between the two films: *The Ladykillers* features a costermonger, Frankie Howerd, mistreating a street horse rather like the one Davies's father, in a photograph and at the stables, is seen looking after.

16 Sarah Whitefield, 'Fragments of an Identical World' (London: Tate Gallery, 1998).

17 In a way that Davies couldn't have known, working on the film in the mid-1980s, this kind of ordinary terraced house has since become a site where art and memory and imagination often meet. In 1993 the sculptor Rachel Whiteread made a concrete cast of the interior of an East End Victorian terrace, newly vacated at 193 Grove Road in Bow, following on from *Ghost,* her casting of a room in Archway, in 1990. More recently, the artist Michael Landy re-created his father's house for *Semi Detached*, which was built inside Tate Britain. The novelist Julie Myerson has written *Home: The Story of Everyone Who Ever Lived in Our House,* chronicling the history of 34 Lillieshall Road in south London. And, perhaps most unpredictably of all, in a television series in the early noughties called *The 1940s House*, a family took part in a four-week experiment, living, eating and breathing in a re-created wartime past for our entertainment.

18 Interview 'Beauty's Slow Fade', *Sight and Sound*, vol. 10 no. 10, October 2000, pp. 14–18.

19 'I came across this amusingly flashy word while researching the subject of the poem. It was coined by an American astrophysicist to describe the act of transforming a barren planet into one capable of sustaining life … 'Eco' comes from the Greek *oikos*, meaning 'a house', while *poesis*, with which the word poetry shares its origins, comes from the Greek meaning 'to make'. Gerard Woodward, *Poetry Book Society Bulletin*, Autumn 2005.

20 Ainsclough's Liverpool photographs, taken in the mid- to late 1960s, probably come closest to Mayne's North Kensington streetscapes of nearly a decade earlier. More generally, the beautiful Liverpool cityscapes of Edward Chambre-Hardman are worth seeking out; Cartier-Bresson photographed in the city too, on a visit to the north of England in 1962; and Snowdon photographed its condemned streets and bad housing, making a *Sunday Times* magazine cover in May, 1970.

21 Interview, 'First Steps in Show Business', Guardian, 6 October 2000.

22 Whereas, according to Dickinson's dictum, nature is a haunted house.

23 Terence Davies, *Hallelujah Now* (London: Brilliance Books, 1984). 'Pain recollected in tranquillity.' This novel is essential reading if you are at all interested in this director's work. Another version of the voyage out, from home in Liverpool to London, then decline, the book is full of detail and imagery that recurs in all of the early films: Annie Gaffney's flowers; rain 'driving in from the Atlantic, from the St. George's Straits way across from Ireland'; Part Two even begins with the shipping forecast. By turns epistolary and lyrical, it has sweep and range; like the earlier films, it explores homosexuality in a less than sympathetic environment, and mortality without a trace of sentimentality.

24 Seamus Heaney, 'Funeral Rites' in *North* (London: Faber and Faber, 1975).

25 Perhaps particularly effective here and in *The Long Day Closes*, because, as Davies told me, this is her period.

26 In Annette Kuhn's *Family Secrets* (London: Verso, 2002), the author at one point describes what I've long experienced as a familiarity with and attraction towards the world we are born into: the point at which personal and collective memory intersect and overlap.

27 Seamus Heaney, 'A Sofa in the Forties' in *The Spirit Level* (London: Faber and Faber, 1996). I realise that I've already mentioned Heaney a couple of times: no one could be more surprised than I am, but there *are* all kinds of chimes and parallels, even down to the insurance man's visit ('A Constable Calls'). Both director and poet seem drawn to, and nourished by, their childhood Edens, and are near contemporaries. And looming over both is Wordsworth: 'Fair seed-time had my soul, and I grew up/Fostered alike by beauty and by fear.'

28 The linguist Kevin Watson talked me through various conference papers on this subject, and explained how reports of scouse's death are greatly exaggerated. For certain phonological features, scouse is resisting external influences where other accents are proving vulnerable because they are more receptive.

29 See his interview in *The Independent*, 6 October 1988: 'Under the angels of Mersey: Terence Davies talks to Kevin Jackson about Liverpool's radio days';

30 and in 'Other Side of the Tracks', *Guardian* 1 July 1989.

31 In her inaugural professorial lecture at Lancaster University 'Living Within the Frame' (2003), Annette Kuhn talked about the fascination this illusion held for early cinemagoers – cinema's distinctive *being*, indeed, as movement of image – and in turn discussed an earlier lecture by the film-maker Laura Mulvey on stillness and the moving image.

32 I mean, of course, Barthes's *Camera Lucida* (New York: Hill and Wang, 1981) and Sontag's *On Photography* (London: Penguin, 1978).

33 Claus Christensen, 'A Vast Edifice of Memories' *p.o.v.*, no. 6, December 1998.

34 The nature of the cinematic zoom into a still photographic image: Michael Snow's 1967 *Wavelength* consists entirely of just this, greatly extended, and its influence in turn has been discerned in films such as *The Shining* (1980), where Kubrick's final shot closes in on an enigma, or *Barton Fink*'s (1991) picture of the ocean that the eponymous blocked writer finally steps into. Still photographs have been used in motion pictures in a number of ways: in Antonioni's *Blow Up* (1966), David Hemming's photographer finds proof of a murder through still contemplation and enlargement; at the end of *Butch Cassidy & the Sundance Kid* (1969), the stilled screen of our two about-to-perish heroes fades slowly into sepia; in Jean-Luc Godard's *JLG/JLG* (1994), a still photograph of Godard as a child is shown as we hear the sounds of kids somewhere at play; and a striking recent example is Andrey Zvyagintsev's *The Return*, from 2004, which uses a series of still images taken during the film's road journey as its coda.

35 In Walter Benjamin's 1931 essay 'A Small History of Photography', in *One-Way Street* (London: Verso, 1979).

36 Robert Bresson, *Notes on the Cinematographer* (London: Quartet, 1986).

37 Geoff Dyer, *The Ongoing Moment* (London: Little, Brown, 2005).

38 From Stevenson's 'Requiem', in *Underwoods*.

39 This also suggests William Blake's 'marriage-hearse'. Blake, of course, also added his own particular rose to the fund of English verse.

40 Robert Frost (1874–1963) once described a poem thus.

41 Sergei Eisenstein, *Film Form* (San Diego: Harcourt, Brace, Jovanovich, 1977).

42 Maya Deren speculated about this relationship at a Cinema 16 symposium 'Poetry and the Film' on 28 October 1953, which exists in transcript. This is a fascinating, sometimes bizarre, document: the other panellists were Parker Tyler, Arthur Miller, Willard Maas and Dylan Thomas, who makes much comedic capital out of Deren's 'horizontal' and 'vertical' notions. *Cinema 16: Documents Towards a History of the Film Society*, ed. Scott MacDonald (Philadelphia: Temple University Press, 2002).

43 Colin McCabe, *The Eloquence of the Vulgar* (London: BFI, 1999).

44 Harlan Kennedy, 'Familiar Haunts', *Film Comment,* vol. 24 no. 5, 1988.

45 Pierre Descargues, *Vermeer* (Geneva: Skira, 1966).

46 André Bazin, *What is Cinema* (Berkley: University of California Press, 1971).

47 Grevel Lindop explained to me how, as a teenager going into the 1960s, he was able to skip school and spend weekdays circulating among Liverpool's fleapits, watching Lon Chaney Jr and Boris Karloff movies. The musicals had gone, and the cinemas' decline anticipated that of the port: liners had stopped docking, cargo was becoming containerised and switching to southern and eastern commercial nodes, and from the middle of the decade onwards tonnage went into a tailspin. 'It took little more than a single decade for Liverpool's port to shrink so much that it became almost unrecognisable. Herman Melville would have still found something to recognise in the mid-1960s, for although ships might have changed, the cargoes they carried and the methods of handling them were sufficiently similar to have been recognisable. By the early 1980s most of the dock system had changed and been converted to other uses.' Tony Lane, *Liverpool: Gateway of Empire* (London: Lawrence and Wishart, 1987). Liverpool's decline and reinvention – especially in terms of its sense of difference and exceptionalism, its early multicultural demographic and meeting-space of diasporas, and its more recent pariah status – would require another book entirely.

48 If the famous scene in *Singin' in the Rain* has a *punctum*, it must be that bright red fire hydrant: this must have looked so strange to 1950s audiences on this side of the Atlantic: a jazz pillar box.

49 D. Petrie (ed.), *Screening Europe* (London: BFI, 1992).

50 Davies has been polled (we know his favourite film is *Singin' in the Rain*, and the nine waiting in line behind it) but also appears in polls: in 2005 Guardian Unlimited asked a panel including Peter Bradshaw, Xan Brooks, Derek Malcolm and Steve Rose for a 'Top 40' style list of the world's best directors. Davies came in at no. 10 – the highest entry for a British director – and this would indicate how his frugal output has done nothing to diminish his work's appeal. This article actually goes on to make some entirely valid complaints about the scandalous difficulties Davies has faced securing funding for his version of Lewis Grassic Gibbon's *Sunset Song*: at the time of writing, a lack of interest (reportedly from the BBC, Channel 4 and the UK Film Council) has meant that the project has been shelved, with a view perhaps to producing a version for television. For all the brouhaha surrounding a re-energised UK film industry, a critically acclaimed director with a number of successful films under his belt and a unique vision can still find himself utterly sidetracked and marginalised. That's showbusiness.

51 Tony Williams, 'Terence Davies: An Interview', *CineAction!*, Summer/Autumn 1990.

52 From 'Nostos', in *Meadowlands* (New York: Ecco, 1997).

53 Joseph Roth, *The Radetzky March,* trans. Michael Hofmann (London: Granta, 2003).

Credits

Distant Voices
Still Lives

UK/West Germany
1988

Directed by
Terence Davies
Producer
Jennifer Howarth
Written by
Terence Davies
Photography
William Diver
Patrick Duval
Editor
William Diver
in collaboration with
Geraldine Creed
Toby Benton
Art Directors
Miki van Zwanenberg
(with Jocelyn James)
Jocelyn James

©Terence Davies

Production Companies
The British Film Institute in
association with Film Four
International presents
A British Film Institute
production in association with
Channel Four Television
Limited and ZDF

Executive Producer
Colin MacCabe
Production Managers
Sarah Swords
Olivia Stewart
Production Accountant
Sheryl Leonardo
Executive in Charge of
Production
Jill Pack
Production Assistants
Olivia Stewart
Lil Stirling
Runners
Ian Francis
George Barbero
Richard Bridgwood
Sholto Roeg
Tony McCaffrey
1st Assistant Directors
[1985] Andy Powell
[1987] Andy Powell
[1987] Glynn Purcell
2nd Assistant Directors
Marc Munden
Mathew Evans
Continuity
Claire Hughes Smith
Melanie Matthews
Casting
Priscilla John
Stunt Photography
Arthur Wooster
Camera Operator
Harriet Cox
Focus Puller
Jeremy Read
Stunt Focus Puller
Martin Kenzie
Clapper Loaders
Maggie Gormley
Caren Moy
Stunt Clapper Loader
Nicholas Penn
Grips
Malcolm Huse
Kevin Fraser
Bill Venables
Nobby Roker
Electricians
Geoff Burlinson
Chris Polden
Gary Nagle
Tim Church

Stunt Electricians
Chris Polden
Gary Willis
Geoffrey Quick
Stills Photographer
Mike Abrahams
Special Effects
Richard Roberts
Editing Assistant
Mick McCarthy
Assistant Art Directors
Sheila Gillie
Mark Stevenson
Standby Props
Dave Allen
Pat Harkins
Construction
Acme Construction:
Colin Rutter
Hank Schumacher
Constructivist:
Susan McLenachan
Alastair Gow
Scenic Artists
Penny Fielding
Joy Fielding
Sarah Thwaites
Painter
Lynne Whiteread
Carpenters
Kevin Huse
Richard Ede
Costume Designer
Monica Howe
Assistant Wardrobe
Simon Murray
Hair and Make-up
Lesley Rouvray-Lawson
Aileen Seaton
Eric Scruby
Jan Archibald
Lesley Sanders
Gerry Jones
Elizabeth Moss
Stunt Make-up
Jenny Shircore
Titles by
Plume Design
Film Laboratory
Metrocolor London Ltd
Lab Supervisors
Ron Barber
Clive Noakes

Camera Equipment
Cine-Europe Ltd
Griphouse
Cinefocus
Lighting Equipment
Film & TV Services
Harmonica
Tommy Reilly
Soundtrack (original)
"Hymn to the Virgin" by
Benjamin Britten and "In the
Bleak Midwinter" by Harold
Darke; Choir Directed by
Simon Preston; Soloist: Mary
Seers
"Love is a Many-Splendoured
Thing" by Sammy Fain and
Paul Francis Webster;
Conducted by David Firman
Orchestrated by Robert
Lockhart
"Pastoral Symphony" by
Vaughan Williams; Soprano:
Susan Bullock
Music Recording Engineers
Antony Howell
Mark Brown
Eric Tomlinson
Soundtrack (pre-existing)
"The Finger of Suspicion" by
Paul Mann and Al Lewis;
published by MCA Music Ltd.;
sung by Dickie Valentine by
kind permission of The Decca
Record Company Ltd.
"Dreamboat" by Jack
Hoffman; published by MCA
Music Ltd.
"I Wanna Be Around", words &
music: Sadie Vimmerstedt and
Johnny Mercer ©Commander
Publications; British publisher:
Warner Bros Music Ltd. used
by kind permission of Warner
Bros Music Ltd.
"O Waly, Waly" performed by
Benjamin Britten and Peter
Pears by kind permission of The
Decca Record Company Ltd.

Sound Recordists
Moya Burns
Colin Nicolson
Boom Operators
Christine Felce
Rupert Castle
Sound Mixers
Aad Wirtz
Ian Turner
Dubbing Editor
Alex Mackie
Assistant Dubbing Editor
Andrew Melhuish
Sound Re-recorded at
Cinelingual Sound Studios Ltd
Ladbroke Films Ltd
Catering
Locaters
Set Meals:
Philip Small
Paul Caldicott
Jutahmart Small
Stunt Co-ordinator
Alf Joint
Stuntman
Bill Weston
Publicity
Liz Reddish
With Special Thanks to
Peter Sainsbury
Mamoun Hassan
The McKee School
A.R.T. Casting
Gill Hallifax
Larry Sider
Max Marrable
Frank Reynolds
David Hill
David Gamble
BBC Sound Archive
National Sound Archive
Denis Norden
Steve Race
Roy Hudd
Gillian Reynolds
Robert Lockhart
Pat Carus
Father Ashworth
Father Thompson

Cast
Freda Dowie
Mrs Davies, mother
Pete Postlethwaite
Tommy Davies, father
Angela Walsh
Eileen
Dean Williams
Tony
Lorraine Ashbourne
Maisie
Sally Davies
Eileen as a child
Nathan Walsh
Tony as a child
Susan Flanagan
Maisie as a child
Michael Starke
Dave, Eileen's husband
Vincent Maguire
George, Maisie's husband
Antonia Mallen
Rose, Tony's wife
Debi Jones
Micky
Chris Darwin
Red
Marie Jelliman
Jingles
Andrew Schofield
Les
Anne Dyson
granny
Jean Boht
Aunty Nell
Alan Bird
baptismal priest
Pauline Quirke
Doreen
Matthew Long
Mr Spaull
Frances Dell
Margie
Carl Chase
Uncle Ted, Tommy's brother
Roy Ford
wedding priest
Terry Melia
John Thomalla
military policemen
John Carr
registrar

John Michie
soldier
Jeanette Moseley
barmaid
Ina Clough
licensee
Chris Benson
Judith Barker
Tom Williamson
Lorraine Michaels
Rose's family

7,523 feet
83 minutes 36 seconds

35mm
Dolby Stereo
In Colour

German title: **Entfernte Stimmen – Stilleben**

Released in UK cinemas on 13 October 1988 by The British Film Institute.

Released in German cinemas on 17 November 1988 by Kinowelt Filmverleih GmbH.

First UK television screening: 4 August 1991 on Channel Four's 'Film on Four' slot.

Filmed in two parts (hence the duplication of several personnel in the credits). 'Distant Voices': Sept to Oct 1985, 'Still Lives': Sept to Oct 1987 on location in London and Liverpool (UK) Budget: £703,000

Also Published

Amores Perros
Paul Julian Smith (2003)

L'Argent
Kent Jones (1999)

Blade Runner
Scott Bukatman (1997)

Blue Velvet
Michael Atkinson (1997)

Bombay
Lalitha Gopalan (2005)

Caravaggio
Leo Bersani & Ulysse Dutoit (1999)

A City of Sadness
Bérénice Reynaud (2002)

Crash
Iain Sinclair (1999)

The Crying Game
Jane Giles (1997)

Dead Man
Jonathan Rosenbaum (2000)

Dilwale Dulhaniya Le Jayenge
Anupama Chopra (2002)

Don't Look Now
Mark Sanderson (1996)

Do the Right Thing
Ed Guerrero (2001)

Easy Rider
Lee Hill (1996)

The Exorcist
Mark Kermode (1997, 2nd edn 1998, rev. 2nd edn 2003)

Eyes Wide Shut
Michel Chion (2002)

Groundhog Day
Ryan Gilbey (2004)

Heat
Nick James (2002)

The Idiots
John Rockwell (2003)

Independence Day
Michael Rogin (1998)

Jaws
Antonia Quirke (2002)

L.A. Confidential
Manohla Dargis (2003)

Last Tango in Paris
David Thompson (1998)

The Matrix
Joshua Clover (2004)

Nosferatu – Phantom der Nacht
S. S. Prawer (2004)

Once Upon a Time in America
Adrian Martin (1998)

Pulp Fiction
Dana Polan (2000)

The Right Stuff
Tom Charity (1997)

Saló or The 120 Days of Sodom
Gary Indiana (2000)

Seven
Richard Dyer (1999)

The Shawshank Redemption
Mark Kermode (2003)

The Silence of the Lambs
Yvonne Tasker (2002)

10
Geoff Andrew (2005)

The Terminator
Sean French (1996)

Thelma & Louise
Marita Sturken (2000)

The Thing
Anne Billson (1997)

The Thin Red Line
Michel Chion (2004)

The 'Three Colours' Trilogy
Geoff Andrew (1998)

Titanic
David M. Lubin (1999)

Trainspotting
Murray Smith (2002)

Unforgiven
Edward Buscombe (2004)

The Usual Suspects
Ernest Larsen (2002)

The Wings of the Dove
Robin Wood (1999)

Withnail & I
Kevin Jackson (2004)

Women on the Verge of a Nervous Breakdown
Peter William Evans (1996)

WR – Mysteries of the Organism
Raymond Durgnat (1999)